CHRIST IS RISEN

Richard Harries
Bishop of Oxford

First published 1987
by A.R. Mowbray & Co. Ltd,
Saint Thomas House, Becket Street,
Oxford, OX1 1SJ

Typeset by Dataset, Oxford
Printed in Great Britain by Cox and Wyman Ltd., Reading

British Library Cataloguing in Publication Data

Harries, Richard, *1936–*
   Christ is risen. — (Mowbray's popular
Christian paperbacks).
   1.   Jesus Christ — Resurrection
   I.   Title
   232'.5   BT 481

ISBN 0–264–67107–4

*To friends and former colleagues
at King's College, London
with thanks for six very happy years*

Publications by Richard Harries

BOOKS

Prayers of Hope BBC 1975
Turning to Prayer Mowbrays 1978
Prayers of Grief and Glory Lutterworth 1979
Being a Christian Mowbrays 1981
(In the USA; *What Christians Believe* Winston Press)
Should a Christian Support Guerillas? Lutterworth 1981
Praying Round the Clock Mowbrays 1983
The Authority of Divine Love Blackwells 1983
Prayer and the Pursuit of Happiness Collins 1985
(In the USA by Eerdmans)
Morning has Broken Marshall Pickering 1985
Christianity and War in a Nuclear Age Mowbrays 1986
C.S. Lewis: The Man and his God Collins 1987

ANTHOLOGIES

Seasons of the Spirit (with George Every and Kallistos Ware) SPCK 1984
(In the USA: *The Time of the Spirit* St. Vladimirs Seminary Press)
The One Genius, Readings through the Year with Austin Farrer SPCK 1987

EDITED AND CONTRIBUTED TO

What Hope in an Armed World? Pickering and Inglis 1982
Reinhold Niebuhr and the Issues of our Time Mowbrays 1986
(In the USA by Eerdmans)

CONTRIBUTED TO

Stewards of the Mysteries of God (ed. E. James) Darton, Longman and Todd, 1975

Unholy Warfare (ed. D. Martin and P. Mullen) Blackwell 1983

The Cross and the Bomb (ed. F. Bridger) Mowbrays 1983

Dropping the Bomb (ed. J. Gladwin) Hodder and Stoughton 1985

Julian, Woman of our Time (ed. R. Llewellyn) Darton, Longman and Todd 1985

'If Christ be not risen . . .' (ed. E. Russell and J. Greenhalgh) St. Mary's, Bourne Street 1986

The Reality of God (ed. J. Butterworth), Severn House 1986

Acknowledgements

I would like to thank two members of the Faculty of Theology and Religious Studies at King's College, London, Dr Francis Watson, Lecturer in New Testament Studies and Dr Christoph Schwöbel, Lecturer in Systematic Theology, who read the typescript and made a number of helpful comments. They are not of course responsible for the judgements I make in this book. I would also like to thank Gillian Ryland for typing the script.

Richard Harries
King's College, London   1987

Contents

1

God's Style

Does it matter?

A Quaker friend once asked me 'Does it really matter whether Jesus rose from the dead? Does it matter whether or not the tomb was empty?' Whether it matters depends on other beliefs we may or may not hold: our belief about God for example and about who we believe Jesus was. If after I died some of my friends claimed to have experienced my continuing spiritual presence with them it would be interesting. If the undertakers also claimed that when they went into the locked and guarded mortuary they found my coffin empty, it would be startling. But neither the discovery of an empty coffin nor the claim of my friends to have experienced my presence would be of earth-shattering importance, though the latter might be adduced as evidence that the human personality survives death. However, in the resurrection of Jesus, much more is involved than that. Why the question of his resurrection matters and is crucial for our whole understanding of life can be seen by recalling four facts basic to any interpretation of the New Testament.

First, Jesus felt himself called by God to announce the imminent presence of the long expected Kingdom of God. Throughout the Old Testament period the Jews, faced with so much evil both in the surrounding nations and within their own society, looked for the time when God himself would act to put right all that was wrong with human life. For much of the time evil was so rampant it seemed that God could not really be the ruler of the world. So they longed for the time when he would show his hand, act decisively, and reveal his just and peaceful rule in human affairs. At the heart of the message of Jesus is the proclamation that this time has come: God's rule is dawning: his kingdom is here. There has, it is true, been much debate amongst New Testament scholars over the last hundred years whether the weight of the message is on the fact that the kingdom is actually present in the person of Jesus or whether it will come very shortly. For our present purpose the outcome of this debate does not matter. Most are agreed that in the New Testament, the rule of God is regarded as already breaking into human affairs in and through Jesus, his message and his miracles. And this conviction derives from Jesus himself. He felt himself called to announce the imminent presence of God's rule in human life and showed through what he said and did that its power to overcome evil was already present.

Secondly, Jesus had a close, intimate relationship with God, whom he called 'Abba' or father. So close was this that he claimed, either explicitly or by implication, to be acting out in his own ministry the pattern of God's action towards human beings. One striking example of this is his response to criticism that he mixed with and had meals with those who were morally and religiously unacceptable. Jesus replied by giving two vivid pictures. One of a shepherd who leaves the bulk of his flock in order to gather in a sheep that has strayed and got lost; the other of a woman who scrabbles all over the floor in order to find a coin she has dropped. In both cases there is great rejoicing when what has been lost is found. 'Just so, I tell you, there is joy before the angels of God over one sinner who repents' (Luke 15, 10). 'The angels of God' is here a respectful way of talking about the heart and mind of God. The implication is clear. What Jesus is doing, going out of his way to be with those who have been pushed out of the enclave of respectable society, is at one with the mind and eternal purpose of God. The pattern of divine action and the pattern of the ministry of Jesus are the same. The one is working out in human terms of what is everlastingly true of God's relationship to human beings.

Thirdly, Jesus put himself totally at the disposal of the one he called 'Abba', whom he taught was utterly trustworthy. According to the Old Testament God is the faithful one. Even though his people Israel go on letting him down he never lets them down. Jesus made this thought his own. He trusted God and God alone, rejecting, as we see in the temptation story (Matthew 4, 1–11), all deviations from what he took to be the father's will. He taught the sheer goodness of God. If human parents, flawed though they are, usually want the best for their children, how much more does God want what is good for us (Luke 11, 13). What he taught he lived out. He gave himself without reserve into the hands and purposes of one he believed to be perfect goodness; he held nothing back from one he trusted would never let him down.

Fourthly, Jesus was rejected and killed. Moreover, he died a death that was not only cruelly painful, it was religiously ignominious. According to Jewish holy law, the Torah, hanging from a tree or crucifixion were accursed forms of death (Deuteronomy 21, 23;

Galatians 3, 13). Jesus, as a good Jew, had looked to the Torah as the revealed will of God. He had pondered it and sought to make its message his own. Through the Torah he had tried to enter into the mind of his heavenly father and obey his holy will. But as a result of that he ended up not only rejected by human beings but cursed by the divine standard he had sought to follow. No wonder he made the opening words of Psalm 22 his own and cried out on the cross 'My God, my God why hast thou forsaken me?' (Mark 15, 34).

If these four points are taken by themselves, with no reference to any other claim, there can be only two conclusions. Either Jesus was mistaken in thinking that he had a special vocation. Or he was mistaken in thinking that God is loving and utterly trustworthy. If I begin to announce that in the year 2000 God will bring the sorry story of humanity to an end and usher in his perfect kingdom and then the year 2000 passes without anything happening, most people would judge that I had been mistaken, that I was suffering from an illusion. This was the general reaction to those who made the same prediction for the year 1000 and to those who throughout human history have made similar claims. So, a natural reaction would be to say that Jesus was mistaken. He misread the mind of God. But a number of facts make the claims of Jesus very different from others who have predicted some great divine shakeup in human history. Above all there has been the almost universal admiration for Jesus's understanding of God as perfect love and for his character as one who reveals, even for the non-Christian, something of that love. In other words our usual reaction to those who make claims about the divine purpose that are not fulfilled is that such people are mistaken in their understanding of God's will but

4

nevertheless there remains a divine purpose, is more difficult in the case of Jesus. His message is so sublime and his character so transparent to his message, that his 'failure' calls into question the basic tenets of his message about God's goodness.

Jesus felt himself called to proclaim the imminent reign of God in human affairs and pointed to his deeds as signs of this reign being inaugurated. He claimed a special intimacy with God as father and suggested that what he was doing was at one with the divine purpose in human history. He taught that this God was utterly trustworthy and committed himself totally to what he understood to be his will. Yet he was not only rejected and killed but condemned by the book which had shaped his life and mission. This 'failure' calls into question not only his claim to be a bringer of the Kingdom but his message that behind the universe there is a power that can be trusted to the uttermost. To put it bluntly, he himself trusted to the bitter end and look where it got him. He lived his life on the basis that a divine goodness animates the universe and a lot of good it did him.

The question then is this. Without the resurrection of Jesus can we really believe that there is a trustworthy love behind human life? A Christian minister was once talking to two Rabbis about their respective beliefs in God. In the course of the conversation the Christian said 'If it wasn't for Jesus I do not think I would even be able to believe in God.' We could go even further than this. Without the resurrection of Jesus would it be possible to believe in God – that is, a God of love who can be trusted? The question of whether or not Jesus rose from the dead is the most important question in human life. For on our answer depends not only the question of whether or not Jesus was mistaken in thinking that he had a special role in the divine purpose but whether or not there is a divine purpose at all. If there was no resurrection there was no special role for Jesus and if he was mistaken in thinking there was a special role for him he is likely to be equally mistaken in his fundamental message about God. No resurrection means no Jesus as the revealer of God's love; and this calls into question whether there is a God of love to be revealed at all. What could be more important than the question whether Jesus was raised from the dead? I know of course there are those, Jews and Muslims amongst them, who believe in a faithful God without believing in Jesus or his resurrection. I just find it difficult for the reasons stated.

What is meant by the resurrection?

For most of Christian history there has been widespread agreement about what was being claimed in saying that God raised Christ Jesus from the dead. The question at issue was whether the claim was true. Did Jesus rise from the dead or not? Yes or no. In recent decades however there has been another, prior question to the fore. What do we mean by the resurrection? For there have been a bewildering variety of interpretations. The question of whether or not Jesus rose from the dead cannot be answered until it is known precisely what it is that is being claimed. In the modern debate there has also been another set of questions lurking. Are all these interpretations legitimate interpretations of the resurrection of Christ? Do they accord with the New Testament view? Are they compatible with Christian orthodoxy? It must be stressed that this last set of questions is outside the scope of this book. What is or is not compatible with historic Christian faith is an important question but it is not one that is being considered here. The various interpretations will be considered simply on their merits without any judgement about what is or is not within the limits of legitimate Christian belief. The position taken in this book will be pursued for its own sake; not because it is either more or less 'orthodox' than other views. Moreover, it is hoped that the arguments with other views will be conducted in the spirit of a poem by Stevie Smith. In this poem whenever the agnostic and the Christian express their doubts about the truth of the opposing view they each assert:

And yet he is more gracious than I,
He has such a gracious personality.[1]

Interpretations of the resurrection of Christ may be placed under four headings. 1. Bodily resuscitation, 2. Bodily transfiguration, 3. Spiritual presence, 4. Mental conversion.

1. *Bodily resuscitation.* This view believes that the tomb was empty and stresses the continuity between the physical body of Jesus during his lifetime and his risen body. It draws particularly on the resurrection stories that have a vivid, down-to-earth quality about them, as in John 21 where Jesus is depicted as standing on the seashore with bread and fish to give his followers, or in John 20 where Thomas can see, and is invited to touch, the very wounds in Christ's body.

The difficulty with this view is that the New Testament lays even greater stress on the discontinuity between the physical body of Jesus during his lifetime and his risen body. The risen Christ comes and goes without physical movement. He is present one moment and gone the next. Above all the New Testament makes it clear that there is an abyss of difference between what happened to Lazarus or the widow of Nain's son. They came back to life in the same form as before; they were once again subject to change and decay and death. Jesus, in contrast, was raised to a new kind of life altogether, no longer subject to the constraints of time and space. He had been raised from the dead to die no more. So it is that St Paul in the famous Chapter 15 of his Letter to the Corinthians emphasizes the radical discontinuity, as well as the continuity, between our physical bodies and what he calls a spiritual body. Although he is writing about the resurrection at the end of time it is clear that he sees here a general principle at work whose exemplar is the resurrection of Christ himself.

> What is sown is perishable, what is raised is imperishable.
> It is sown in dishonour, it is raised in glory.
> It is sown in weakness, it is raised in power.
> It is sown a physical body, it is raised a spiritual body . . .
>
> We shall not all sleep, but we shall all be changed . . .
> For this perishable nature must put on the imperishable,
> and this mortal nature must put on immortality.

According to Paul then, Christ was raised in a new form, to a new kind of life altogether. He was not simply resuscitated from the dead as Lazarus had been. He was raised imperishable and immortal; transfigured into a spiritual body made of the very stuff of glory.

2. *Bodily transfiguration*. This view that the body of Jesus was transmuted into a substance appropriate to an eternal

form of existence does justice to St Paul's teaching in Corinthians 15 and to the element of discontinuity between the physical body of Jesus and his risen presence in the resurrection appearances. The difficulties with this view are of three rather different kinds all of which need to be considered.

First, there is the question whether such an astounding miracle could possibly happen. Our modern mind set is highly sceptical about such supernatural events. Faced with the story of the empty tomb we look instinctively for a natural explanation. Secondly, there is the status of the empty tomb stories themselves. For it is widely believed by modern New Testament scholars that the empty tomb tradition is late, in New Testament terms, and grew up some years after the stories about appearances of the risen Christ had circulated. It is claimed that there are discrepancies in the stories themselves that cannot be reconciled and that, above all, there is no mention of the finding of the empty tomb in our earliest account of the resurrection tradition. In 1 Corinthians 15, 1–8 Paul recounts the evidence for the resurrection. That at least some of what he recalls is much earlier than Paul himself is indicated by the technical terms he uses for passing on a tradition. In that passage he recounts a number of appearances of the risen Christ. But he does not mention anything about women going to the tomb and finding it empty. Indeed he does not mention a tomb at all. St Paul wrote 1 Corinthians about the year AD. 54. So in referring there to a tradition that he had received much earlier we have here a statement of Christian belief that goes back to the years immediately after the resurrection itself. But there is no mention of the empty tomb.

The third question is of a rather different kind. When the controversy about the Bishop of Durham's views on the Virgin Birth (more accurately called the virginal conception) first raged I was having a meal with a composer who is also a thoughtful Christian. Referring to the belief that Jesus was conceived by a virgin through the agency of the Holy Spirit he asked 'Is it God's style?' In other words we can recognise Chopin or Mahler or Bach by the style of their music and when we hear an unknown work we try to guess the composer by what we know of various styles. What is God's style? How does he achieve his purposes in the world and does, for example, being conceived of a virgin fit into that style? Is it congruous with what we understand to be his way of working? There is a challenge here not only to belief in the Virgin Birth but to the bodily transfiguration of Jesus. For if we leave out the healing miracles, which Christ performed out of compassion for the sufferers, it is quite clear from the Gospels that he rejected the idea of gaining people's allegiance by working miracles for them. Furthermore, he rejected all suggestions that he might deploy heavenly power in order to escape his own destiny of suffering. The story of the temptation in the wilderness shows Christ choosing the way of trust rather than wonder working. The incident in the Garden of Gethsemane shows him going through with the way of suffering rather than the way of force, either human or divine.

> Do you think that I cannot appeal to my Father, and he will at once send me more than twelve legions of angels? But how then should the scriptures be fulfilled, that it must be so? (Matthew 25, 53–4)

If Jesus, who reveals to us the mind of God, deliberately rejects all ways of winning a following by overpowering displays of divine power, what are we to make of a resurrection which seems just that? Does it not seem out of character, out of keeping with what Jesus has revealed as the road of suffering? Is it God's style?

3. *Spiritual presence.* According to this view there is no essential connection between the physical body of Jesus in his historical ministry and his spiritual presence with us now. On the older versions of this view stress would be laid on the soul or essential self of Jesus who appeared to his followers immediately after his death. On modern variations this soul or essential self would also be, or be clothed with, a spiritual body as indicated by St Paul in 1 Corinthians 15. But the essential difference between both these variants and the previous approach discussed here, which thinks in terms of a transfigured body, is that there is no necessary connection between the earthly body and his risen spiritual presence. The two can and do exist apart from one another. To put it bluntly, the earthly body rots and becomes part of the earth. The newly created or recreated spiritual body, which is the essential self of Jesus clothed in a form and manner appropriate to an eternal form of existence, lives for ever as a spiritual presence.

The advantage of this interpretation is that it allows for what many, if not all, New Testament scholars believe, namely the priority in time of the tradition of resurrection appearances over the story of the empty tomb. On this view all weight falls on the resurrection appearances and this is precisely where many New Testament scholars say that it should fall from a historical point of view. A further advantage is that the resurrection of Christ and our resurrection have the same pattern. For in so far as we can know about these things our bodies disintegrate and become part of the earth. We do not now envisage the physical corpuscles of these earthly bodies being gathered

11

together and renewed so that we can climb out of our graves on Doomsday like characters in a Stanley Spencer painting. What we believe for ourselves, if we believe in the resurrection of the body at all, is that our real self, known only to God, is clothed with a form of expression appropriate to an eternal existence. According to the view of the resurrection of Christ which sees it in terms of a spiritual presence, this is precisely what happened to Christ himself.

There are however three questions which have to be pressed against this interpretation. First, it is no less miraculous than the second interpretation, that which posits a transfigured body. It requires no less of a supranatural act to clothe the self out of nothing than it does to transfigure already existing material into a spiritual body. So all the questions about miracles are raised in relation to this approach just as much as the previous one. Secondly, if we accept the historicity of the story of the burial there is the plain man's question about what happened to the body. Jesus had a body and something happened to it. If it was not transmuted into the stuff of eternity it remained, and remains, on earth. One wonders why it was never found either by the enemies or the friends of the first Christians. Thirdly, under the heading of 'God's style' there is the question of God's attitude to the whole material order. According to the book of Genesis God said about the physical world that he had made 'And behold, it was very good'. The Christian church, from its earliest days, sharply distinguished its own beliefs from those many alternative views abroad in the ancient world which put a huge wedge between the spiritual and the physical. All forms of dualism between the material and the spiritual were rejected. Human beings were affirmed to be a unity of body and spirit and life in all its aspects, physical as well as spiritual, social as well as private, were affirmed as important. Bishop Charles Gore used to speak of 'The wonderful coherence of Christian doctrine'. If the body of Jesus was simply sloughed off at death, like a snake discarding an old skin, the body in which he lived and suffered and loved, is this congruous with the very positive evaluation of the material conveyed by the rest of Christian belief?

4. *Mental conversion.* On this view the focus is not so much on what did or did not happen to the body of Jesus but on what happened in the hearts and minds of his followers. In essence they came to see his life and death in a new light, as a triumph instead of a disaster and this 'seeing' is a seeing of the risen Lord. Whether suddenly through a flash of insight or gradually through long meditation on the facts of Jesus and his death, they came to 'see'; to see that death as victorious, not a defeat but a victory for love. There are variants on this view depending on whether this 'seeing' or re-evaluation of the facts of Jesus has some correspondence in an objective world or whether it is a purely subjective experience. But either way the advantages and disadvantages of this view are clear enough. The advantages are that it does not depend on anything that in normal usage would be termed miraculous. Furthermore, it is an interpretation that is compatible with any historical findings about both the empty tomb and the appearance stories. What is decisive is what occurred in the hearts and minds of the disciples; the stories may simply express and reflect this change.

The main advantage or appeal of this view however is that it has a moral quality, almost a heroic quality, that might make it appear more than any other view congruous with 'God's style'. For here is no *Deus ex machina*, a God appearing from behind the scenes at the last moment to put right everything that has previously gone wrong. Here is no happy ending tacked on at the end of a disturbing but haunting tragedy. Here are the disciples, through their own moral and spiritual insight, coming to see the love displayed in Jesus, even in death, above all in death, as a supreme triumph of the human spirit. Through coming to see that and through committing themselves to live by what he personified, Jesus is indeed risen. It is a view with great moral and spiritual attractiveness. The main question raised against this interpretation is whether, despite its almost heroic moral quality, it can sustain rational belief in a God of love. For it would be quite possible on this view for an atheist to come to 'see' Jesus risen in the way described, without any corresponding belief in God or the hope that one day the objective world will indeed be transformed so that in its entirety, outwardly and inwardly, it displays the divine love. Human history is, thank God, studded with the jewels of martyrs, with those who have given their lives for some noble cause. Such lives inspire us; we can have hope that they are not lives sacrificed in vain. But can such lives by themselves give us any confidence that the universe is on the side of the values for which they died? In June 1986 there were a number of 'celebrations' of the 1976 Soweto uprising and the lives of the children who perished in it. The children who were killed because they dared to stand up can be an inspiration. We can have hope that in God they will be raised to fullness of life in the kingdom of God. Yet the hard and tragic fact is that they are dead, killed in their youth with their potentiality unfulfilled. In the actual world in which we now live oppression and brutality reign. Bullets entered their bodies and they died. The life and death of Jesus can be understood in the same way as we understand the lives and deaths of those children, as an inspiration and a hope. But if understood in that way can it give us any real confidence that the universe is on the side of value? That the belief for which Jesus lived and died, that there is a loving power behind the universe, is more than wishful thinking? We all engage in wishful thinking. But the claim of the first Christians was that something objective had occurred, something in the world of events, something in history. Professor Donald Mackinnon has written:

> For the Christian as much as for the Marxist there
> is a sense in which deed takes precedence over idea;
> or rather, idea is significant only as expressed in
> action.

The Christian, like the Marxist, will rightly be suspicious of ideas that float above reality. The Marxist is concerned with what happens in the actual world, the world of suffering and struggle, of politics and economics. So is the Christian. It is because the Christian has confidence that a deed was actually wrought in the world we know, that one who was dead was raised to life, that a tomb was found empty, that there is hope for the martyrs and for us all.

This is not to say that the resurrection of Christ can be 'proved' by providing apparently incontrovertible historical evidence. It will become clear as this book develops that the resurrection of Christ is part of a total vision of God and life, and can only be properly considered as part of that whole. Nevertheless, the question about its historical basis remains important. If a person comes home after watching a football match enthusing how well their team has played and what a

15

sensational victory it was, but then under questioning they disclose that their team did not actually score any goals, the whole account would be undermined. On the other hand, independent evidence that the side did score some goals, whilst it would not prove that they had played well or even won the match, would open up the possibility of these claims being true.

Miracles

There is a basic presupposition shared by many people in the modern world that 'miracles just do not happen'. People believe that science has somehow ruled them out. Of course people mean different things by the word miracle. The poet Walt Whitman wrote that he knew nothing but miracles, meaning that every ordinary experience was miraculous; and there is truth in that view, if the created order is itself the supreme miracle. In this book, here and in chapter 5 where the discussion is continued, the word miracle is used in the old fashioned popular sense to indicate an event that cannot be explained by what are at present known of the laws of nature and indeed which seems to contradict them. (The laws of nature are observed regularities on the basis of which we can make reliable predictions about the future.) The belief that miracles, in this sense, 'just don't happen' is a presupposition, not an assertion that has been or ever could be proved. Secondly, it is not a presupposition that could be shared by any Christian. For according to Christian belief God created the world *ex nihilo*, out of nothing. In the light of that supreme miracle everything (except that which is by definition contradictory) is possible. The real question for a religious believer is not whether God could work miracles, for of course he can, but whether he does;

whether this is the way in which he chooses to work his purpose in the world. It is here that the real difficulty arises, which is not a scientific difficulty but a religious one, that is, one which concerns our whole understanding of God. For it is quite clear on both Biblical and general historical grounds that God chooses, for the most part, to work his purpose through the ordinary course of nature and the free co-operation of human beings.

In order for rational human beings to exist at all there must be a stable, predictable environment. An Alice in Wonderland world, where miracles were happening all the time, would make it impossible for rationality to survive for long. So, because God has chosen to bring about creatures that share his own rationality, he has set us in an impersonal environment, one in which everything goes its own way in a manner that is in principle predictable. This environment often seems hard; floods, earthquakes and volcanoes sweep away good and evil alike. But this impersonal hardness of nature is in fact an aspect of the predictability and therefore the faithfulness of God. 'For he makes his sun rise on the evil and on the good, and sends rain on the just and the unjust' (Matthew 5, 45).

Given this faithfulness of God working through the regularity of nature, a regularity without which it would not be possible for rational human minds to exist, how can we countenance the possibility of God working in ways which contradict the observed and predictable 'laws' of nature? So far as we know about these things – and we are here exploring the deepest of mysteries, the Divine mind and purpose – it is that God wants us to have an assurance and confidence about life. He wants us to have the conviction that God is indeed God, that God is on the side of love and that love cannot be defeated. He reveals his very self, his heart of love, in Christ and through the resurrection assures us that this love will prove triumphant.

Oddly, many people in our time are reluctant to respond to a message that gives hope and confidence. This is partly because there is a genuine moral appeal in a tragic view of the universe. The picture of mankind asserting moral values in a tragic and finally meaningless world has a nobility about it which often seems morally superior to unrealistic and superficial forms of optimism. But there also seems to be something in ourselves which is somewhat less healthy; a kind of inner defeat which wants everything to be defeated and tragic. It is this which makes us sometimes reluctant to respond to a view of the universe which offers a final victory over evil and death. And although there are many forms of unfounded, arrogant and insensitive confidence, the Christian faith puts before the world the pledge of a love that will win through, a divine love whose ultimate victory has been anticipated in the life, death and resurrection of Jesus Christ.

For a God who created the world out of nothing, miracles are certainly possible. And although it is the will of God to achieve his purpose in almost every circumstance through the ordinary processes of nature and human co-operation, this being a reflection of his consistency and faithfulness, there could be an occasion for a supreme miracle. The purpose of such a miracle would be to continue the process of redemption, set in motion by the incarnation, leading to the liberation of all those willing to be liberated; liberated, that is, from sin and death and raised to eternal life with God now and forever. But did such a supreme miracle happen? We first examine the claim that on the third day, the tomb where Jesus's body had been laid to rest, was found empty.

For there are people who are in principle prepared to accept the possibility of miracle but who are sceptical about particular miracles because of the number of miracle stories that have come down to us from the ancient world that they find impossible to believe. If so many miracle stories are obviously legendary, then why should we believe the story of the resurrection of Jesus? A detailed examination of the evidence is necessary.

2

The Empty Tomb

Paul's Evidence

A widely held view amongst New Testament scholars is that the story of some women going to the tomb of Jesus and finding it empty is relatively late, much later, that is, than the tradition that the risen Lord appeared to his followers. Some scholars would take the further step and say it is not only late but legendary. The disciples of Jesus knew that their master had risen, for they had experienced his presence. The story of the empty tomb was a consequence of this faith; invented to express that belief and to account for the fact that one whom they knew to have lived a physical life and died a physical death was now alive. There are two main reasons for this scepticism; first the fact that the empty tomb story is not referred to in the earliest evidence for the resurrection and secondly, apparent inconsistencies in the accounts of the finding of the empty tomb.

The earliest evidence for the resurrection is 1 Corinthians 15, 3–5. There St Paul wrote:

> For I delivered to you as of first importance what I also received, that Christ died for our sins in accordance with the scriptures, that he was buried,

that he was raised on the third day in accordance with the scriptures, and that he appeared to Cephas, then to the twelve.

As already mentioned, 1 Corinthians was written about the year 54. But the tradition recounted in this passage is much older, for the words 'delivered' and 'received' are semi-technical terms for the passing on of an oral tradition. St Paul is referring here to a statement that goes back to the earliest years after the crucifixion of Christ. But this account nowhere refers to the discovery of the empty tomb. It is this lack which has made some scholars think the story of the empty tomb to be late and legendary, the product of faith rather than one of its foundations. What are we to make of this judgement?

First, although there is no mention of the empty tomb it seems quite clear that Paul himself believed in the resurrection of the physical body of Jesus. In 1 Corinthians 15, 4 he refers to the burial of Jesus (see also Romans 6–4). Later in that chapter, where Paul discusses the resurrection of Christians, he is thinking in terms of a physical body. There is, he suggests, discontinuity between our 'spiritual body' and our present physical body but there is also continuity. The relationship between the two is as between a seed and the full grown plant. What is sown as perishable and physical is raised as imperishable and spiritual. But the one is raised out of the other, not from somewhere else altogether. Other references could be cited that make the same point. For example, Paul compares Christian baptism with being buried with Christ, 'so that as Christ was raised from the dead by the glory of the Father, we too might walk in newness of life'.

There is little doubt that Paul himself believed that the physical body of Jesus which had been buried had been raised and changed into an imperishable spiritual body. But does the phrase 'he was raised on the third day in accordance with the scriptures' carry an implicit reference to the empty tomb story? The reference to 'on the third day', or the Markan equivalent 'after three days', is very solidly established in the tradition. This is somewhat surprising. For, except for Matthew's imaginative embellishment, the Gospel writers do not attempt to explore the mystery of *when* the body of Jesus was raised. They simply assume it took place at some time before the women arrived at the tomb. Furthermore, the references to resurrection happening on the third day in the Old Testament are hardly numerous. There was the reference, picked up by Matthew, to Jonah being in the belly of the whale three days and three nights and, more influential on New Testament writers, Hosea 6, 1–2:

> Come, let us return to the Lord; for he has torn, that he may heal us; he has stricken, and he will bind us up. After two days he will revive us; on the third day he will raise us up, that we may live before him.

Later Jewish writers and perhaps some in the time of Jesus saw in this a reference to the resurrection of the dead and it is clearly a passage with great depth of spiritual meaning. But is it really enough to give birth to the fundamental affirmation 'he was raised on the third day *according to the scriptures*'? It would seem rather that there is something about 'on the third day', some historical reminiscence, which made the first Christians look to the Old Testament for some anticipation of it. This historical reminiscence can hardly be to the resurrection appearances, for there is no stress on these happening on the third day. On the contrary, they are spread over a long period of time. It would seem then that it is the discovery of the empty tomb 'on the first day of the week' that underlies the tradition that something decisive happened on the third day. It was not the resurrection itself, which is hidden in the mystery of God, or the appearances, but the discovery of the tomb empty which gave rise to the formula about being raised on the third day and which set Christians looking to the Old Testament to find an anticipation of this.

Nor is there any fundamental opposition between the formula 'on the third day' and the Gospel writers' reference to 'on the first day of the week'. The latter is the natural way of describing the event from the point of view of those who witnessed it. The former is equally natural for a summary of the Christian message.

The evidence suggests that the earliest tradition contained an implicit reference to the finding of the tomb empty on the third day. If Paul received this tradition why did he not recount the empty tomb story in full?

Two points can be made. First, it seems that the evidence of women was not regarded as totally reliable and was not allowed in a court of law. This, as we shall see, makes the existence of the empty tomb tradition witnessed to by women all the more remarkable. But St Paul's attitude to women was somewhat negative and he himself may have been reluctant to accept their testimony. Secondly, and more important however, in 1 Corinthians 15 Paul is not marshalling all the evidence for the resurrection of Christ. He is tackling the disbelief of some readers in the general resurrection of Christians. Furthermore, concerned as he is with his own authority as an apostle, it is only natural that he should concentrate on that part of the evidence for the resurrection which corresponds to his own experience. He himself had encountered Christ on the road to Damascus. He regards this appearance of the risen Christ as being in the same category as the other appearances; 'Last of all, as to one untimely born, he appeared also to me.' All use of evidence is selective. This is not necessarily dishonest. There is usually a multiplicity of facts and some kind of selection and arrangement is necessary. That selection and arrangement inevitably reflects our own experience, standpoint and interests. Paul's apostleship was sometimes called into dispute. First hand witness to the resurrection was accepted as a crucial criterion of apostolic authority. Paul had not been to the empty tomb. He had probably not met the women who had. On the other hand he, like the other apostles, had encountered the risen Christ in an overwhelming spiritual experience. It was only natural that he should focus on this. But in focusing on this he may, knowingly or unknowingly, have left out of account other, somewhat different traditions about evidence for the resurrection that were circulating in some parts of the church.

The Gospel Accounts

The second reason why some New Testament scholars are inclined to take the empty tomb story as late and legendary is because of apparent differences and inconsistencies in the various accounts. For example in Mark and Luke three women go to the tomb, in Matthew two women go and in John only Mary Magdalene goes (though later she says, '*we* do not know where they have laid him'). The reason for going to the tomb also varies. In John and Matthew no reason is given but in Mark and Luke we are told the women went in order to anoint the body of Jesus. But if they were going to anoint the body why did they not take someone with them to roll away the stone?

One popular theory amongst New Testament scholars is that a simple story about women coming to the tomb was developed over the years for apologetic purposes, reaching its most sophisticated form in John 20. There is no doubt that there has been some development of the story with a view to refuting allegations made against the Christian church. The reference in Matthew to a guard being set over the tomb would seem to fall into this category. But it is by no means obvious that the account in John is to be seen in these terms as the latest step in a series of developments. And this makes a difference as to how the empty tomb story is assessed. On one view we have a basic story (in Mark) that has been elaborated over the years to meet criticisms made against the church. On the other view we have two accounts of the finding of the empty tomb (that in Mark and that in John) circulating from an early stage. Some years ago C.H. Dodd argued that in John's Gospel there were genuine historical traditions that had been handed down independently of the synoptic Gospels. More recently John Robinson argued that the Gospel of John, or at least many of its historical traditions, go back to a primal source, the apostle John himself. Using both the synoptics and Johannine traditions then, what historical basis do we find?

To the Christian claim that the tomb of Jesus had been visited and found empty many obvious rejoinders can be made and were made. First, it can be doubted whether the women had visited the correct tomb. One possibility is that the body of Jesus was simply thrown into a common grave for malefactors and became there indistinguishable from any other corpse. But the New Testament tells a very different story. It says that Joseph of Arimathea pleaded with Pilate for the body of Jesus and supervised his burial in a tomb cut in the rock. Nearly, though not quite all, New Testament scholars believe that the story of Joseph of Arimathea is grounded in historical fact. Nor is there anything implausible about Pilate granting such a request. Joseph was not just anybody, but a person of influence. Jesus was a striking prophet who had made a great stir. The Gospel stories reflect a tradition that even Pilate himself had been touched and troubled by him. Given the great veneration which his followers had for Jesus, and the importance attached to reverent burial, it makes total sense to envisage someone sympathetic to the message of Jesus, and a man of influence, trying to recover and bury the body. This is the account of Mark and it is corroborated by what may be an independent tradition in John. John's account is simpler than Mark's (often taken by New Testament scholars as a sign of authenticity). It does however contain some details that have given rise to suspicion, for example, the mention of Nicodemus, the huge amount of spices that were prepared, the new tomb in the garden and so on. But John Robinson argued that these details in fact serve to authenticate the story. The name Nicodemus, for example, was a well known one in Jerusalem at the time and attached to persons of eminence and wealth. The son and grandson of Nicodemus are mentioned by Josephus the Jewish historian. The spices were not for the anointing of the body (the purpose for which, according to Mark, the women went to the tomb) but to preserve the body from putrefaction and keep it smelling sweet over the Sabbath. Spices in powdered and granule form were laid under the corpse and packed around it. Large quantities could be used. At the funeral of Herod the Great there were 500 servants carrying spices. The spices were an expression of the generosity of a rich man, his last tribute to Jesus. As for the location of the tomb, the existence of gardens outside the North wall of the city was known to Josephus, as was the custom of burial in one's own garden.

All four Gospels record that some of the women who followed Jesus watched the crucifixion. Mark, Matthew and Luke go on to say that at least a few of these women saw where Jesus was buried. They then continue with the story of women finding the tomb empty. In other words, Jesus really died, was really buried, and knowing where he was buried the women went to the correct tomb. Doubts have been raised about the Gospel accounts of this sequence at a number of points. First, the names of the women vary. For example in Mark it is Mary Magdalene and 'Mary the mother of Joses' who saw where Jesus was laid. But earlier it had been Mary Magdalene, 'Mary the mother of James the younger and of Joses' and Salome who had watched the crucifixion from afar. Later, at the visit to the tomb, it is Mary Magdalene, 'Mary the mother of James' and Salome. It has been suggested that we have here evidence of two independent traditions, one recounting the passion and burial and the other the finding of the tomb, which have been roughly stitched together by Mark. Yet if Mark's purpose was primarily that of refuting allegations that the wrong tomb had been visited, he could easily have stitched his material together with greater consistency. The fact that Salome did not watch the burial but was in the group that visited the tomb may be just one of those details which are genuine because they do not serve some tidy propaganda pattern.

The second reason for doubting the empty tomb story concerns the motive for the women going to the tomb. In the accounts of Mark and Luke they go to anoint the body of Jesus. This reason is to be taken with the earlier story of a woman who had anointed Jesus with expensive ointment whilst he was still alive, an event which is interpreted as an anointing beforehand. Behind this 'anointing beforehand' was a recollection that there had not been time to wash the body of Jesus with the scented soaps and oils before burial. In Matthew on the other hand, the women go simply 'to see the sepulchre'. For Matthew this could be the only possible motive because according to him the tomb is sealed and guarded. But John also has no mention of going to anoint the body of Jesus. So why were the women going to the tomb? John's account of the burial of the body by Joseph and Nicodemus with a large quantity of myrrh and aloes does not exclude anointing. The two were different processes. As has already been mentioned, the spices used by Joseph and Nicodemus were to pack under and round the body to stop putrefaction. The anointing was the washing of the body with scented soap and oils. The short time left on the Friday after the crucifixion before the Sabbath began could have left time for the one and not for the other longer process.

Yet even if the notion that the women came to the tomb to anoint the body is not firmly established, it was entirely natural that they should visit the tomb to mourn. Mourning played a highly important part in Jewish society at that time and there is some evidence that the third day of mourning was regarded as the peak.

Linked with the question of motive for visiting the tomb is the matter of the large stone that had been rolled in front of its entrance. If the women had indeed set out with the intention of going into the tomb in order to anoint the body would they not have taken a man along with them to help remove the stone? In John, however, the question 'Who will roll away the stone for us from the door of the tomb?' is not raised, because he does not state that they are going to anoint the body.

Despite the difficulties of detail there are two general considerations in favour of the primitive nature of the empty tomb tradition. First, there is the testimony of all four Gospels that when the women arrived at the tomb they found the stone rolled back. This fact is somewhat of an embarrassment for the Christian case, for it immediately prompts the idea that someone was at the tomb before the women and it was they who removed the body. This is the first thought that occurs to us, as it was the first explanation to occur to Mary in the Fourth Gospel and to the opponents of the church generally. Assuming for the moment the women had indeed come to anoint the body, they would have taken a man along with them and he would have rolled back the stone. They would then have gone into the tomb and found it empty. Such a sequence would at least not raise so immediately the thought that someone had reached the tomb before the women and taken the body. Furthermore, the moving of the stone, far from being a help to believing in the resurrection of Christ, is a problem for another reason. If the body of Jesus was changed into an imperishable spiritual body it certainly did not need the stone removing in order to escape from the tomb. Both Luke and John make it quite clear that the risen Christ was not bounded by space. He appeared and disappeared at will without needing to go in and out of doors. Matthew overcomes the embarrassment of the rolled away stone by attributing the movement to an earthquake and the appearance of an angel. But if this is regarded as dramatic embellishment to the story rather than history, the embarrassment of the rolled away stone remains. It was not needed for the proclamation that Christ was risen and it invited the suggestion that someone had stolen the body. So, whatever explanation may be given of the empty tomb, the reference to a stone discovered already rolled back has the stubborn insistence of fact about it.

The second general consideration is that all the Gospels agree it was women who discovered the tomb empty. As has already been mentioned, the testimony of women was not regarded as totally reliable and was not accepted in a court of law. It is all the more remarkable therefore that the earliest empty tomb tradition rests on the testimony of women, and women alone. If the story had been invented for propaganda purposes, as an expression of resurrection faith, it is reasonable to suppose that men would have been given a more prominent role.

The evidence suggests therefore that the story of the empty tomb, far from being late, was in circulation from the first days of the Christian church. This story in its original forms probably consisted of four elements:

1) Mary Magdalene and two or more women went to the tomb of Jesus.
2) They discovered the stone rolled back and the tomb empty.
3) A young man or angel explained 'He is raised: he is not here'.
4) The women go away fearful.

The existence of the empty tomb by itself proves nothing. Indeed opponents of the Christian church might from the first have accepted the empty tomb but put forward their own interpretation of what happened, namely, that the body was stolen. So, from the first, the Christian interpretation of what happened was woven into the story through the message of an angel. Angels in the Old Testament are a natural way of talking about messages from God. And the women may indeed have had some overwhelming spiritual experience in which they learnt of the Lord's resurrection from an angel. The point is, however, whatever they experienced, the earliest telling of the story included what was believed to be a God-given interpretation of the empty tomb.

Whether or not the Christian interpretation of the empty tomb is true – that Christ is risen – the story of its discovery is not only early but has about it the cragginess of fact. Far from being late and legendary it is early and authentic. As the Jewish scholar Geza Vermes has written:

> But in the end, when every argument has been considered and weighed, the only conclusion acceptable to the historian must be that the opinions of the orthodox, the liberal sympathizer and the critical agnostic alike – and even perhaps the disciples themselves – are simply interpretations of the one disconcerting fact: namely that the women who set out to pay their last respects to Jesus found to their consternation, not a body, but an empty tomb.[2]

The discovery of the empty tomb by itself does not prove that Christ is risen. It is a disconcerting fact that needs interpreting. A fuller discussion of this must await the chapter on fact and interpretation but some preliminary points can be made here.

First, Jesus really died. D.H. Lawrence wrote a story in which Jesus was not fully killed by the crucifixion. He

31

regained consciousness in the tomb, struggled out and went eventually to live with a priestess of Isis. The Gospels suggest that Jesus died relatively quickly and are at pains to point out that he was indeed dead when taken down from the cross. According to Mark the reality of his death was affirmed by one of Pilate's centurions, and there is nothing intellectually improbable about this. The latest medical analysis, published in the *Journal of the American Medical Association* argues that Jesus died from blood loss and the shock brought on by the scourging. People crucified tended to survive between three to four hours and three to four days. The relatively rapid death of Jesus suggests that he was indeed severely scourged and this may help to explain why he was too weak to carry the cross bar. On the cross the weight of the body hanging from the arms made it virtually impossible for a victim to exhale fully. This, combined with the shock and blood loss due to the severe scourging, quickly brought about the death of Jesus.

Secondly, he was buried and the whereabouts of his tomb were known to Joseph of Arimathea and the intimate women friends of Jesus. As was argued earlier, the story of Joseph of Arimathea is unlikely to have been invented.

Thirdly, Mary Magdalene and some other women went to the tomb – probably to mourn though perhaps also to wash and anoint the body – and discovered to their surprise the stone rolled away and the tomb empty. The obvious explanations of this disturbing fact are:

1) The opponents of Jesus stole the body. Yet none of them ever produced it. The Christian claim that Jesus was risen would have collapsed instantaneously if those opposed to the message of the young church had produced the corpse of Jesus. But they failed to do so.

2) A disciple stole the body. This raises various questions. What would the motive have been? If it was to erect a special tomb so that there might be a holy place for this great prophet, there remains the fact that there is no evidence of a revered tomb until Helena, the mother of the emperor Constantine, discovered what she believed to be the Holy places in the 4th century. Then there is the question of the psychological state of the disciples. In their broken, shocked, demoralised state of mind, would they have undertaken such a risky task as stealing the body of a condemned criminal? At this stage it can be said that the obvious explanations of the empty tomb raise more questions than they answer. The tomb was discovered empty. This is the disconcerting fact that remains to be interpreted.

3

Appearances of the Risen Lord

The New Testament records a number of appearances of the risen Lord to his followers. Only four are considered here. The appearance to Peter, the appearance to 'the twelve', the appearance to Mary Magdalene and the appearance to Paul on the road to Damascus. These four are selected because the evidence for them seems solid and because of their intrinsic interest. They reveal something of what it is that we are dealing with when we talk about 'an appearance'.

An Appearance to Peter

In the oldest tradition about the resurrection of Christ, Paul wrote about Jesus 'that he was raised on the third day in accordance with the scriptures, and that he appeared to Cephas.' Cephas is the Aramaic name for rock and Aramaic was the language which Jesus spoke. He does not say where this appearance took place but he does place it first in his list. Luke records that when the two disciples who encountered Jesus on the road to Emmaus returned to Jerusalem they found the eleven who said to them, 'The Lord has risen indeed, and has appeared to Simon'. However, there are doubts about Luke's placing of the resurrection appearances in

Jerusalem and questions about whether that verse was part of the original narrative or an independent tradition that has become incorporated in the story in that form. The angel in Mark's account says to Mary Magdalene, 'But go, tell his disciples and Peter that he is going before you to Galilee; there you will see him, as he told you.' (Mark 16, 7). The apocryphal *Gospel of Peter* also records the appearance to Peter in Galilee, though he places it later. Finally there is the strange, dramatic story in John 21 which records the appearance of the risen Christ to a group of disciples on the Lake of Galilee, a story in which Peter is particularly prominent.

There are several signs in the account of John 21 which suggest it is the record of a first appearance to Peter. Peter has gone fishing. This return to his old job would hardly make sense if he had already met and been commissioned by the risen Lord. Then Peter's failure to recognise Christ and his initial response suggest a first encounter rather than a subsequent one. Finally the threefold question to Peter, 'Do you love me?' and Peter's anguished affirmation that he does, which is to be seen as a rehabilitation of Peter as a disciple corresponding to the threefold denial, are more likely to have occurred on the first encounter with the risen Lord.

It is possible that John 21 contains two resurrection stories that must have been run together, the appearance to a group of disciples connected with the meal, and the appearance to Peter. Yet if we have here a record of the risen Christ's first appearance to Peter and this appearance was placed first in the tradition transmitted by Paul why does it not appear in narrative form in the other Gospels? Many scholars argue that it does but in disguised form. Three stories in particular may have, lying behind them, an account of the risen Lord's appearance to Peter.

1) Matthew 14, 28–33. The disciples are in the boat and see Christ coming towards them. Peter begins to walk towards Christ but begins to sink and calls out for Christ to save him. He is rebuked for his lack of faith and the disciples confess Christ as Son of God.
2) Matthew 16, 6–19, the confession by Peter that Jesus is the Christ and the words to Peter that he is the rock on which the church will be built. Peter is given the keys, a symbol of authority.
3) Luke 5, 1–11. Here there are many parallels with the account in John 21. The disciples have fished all night and caught nothing. Jesus tells them to put out the nets for a catch. A large catch is made. Peter is the one who reacts to the catch and Jesus is called Lord. The theme of following Jesus occurs and the catch of fish symbolises a successful missionary endeavour.

It is difficult to see why an incident that occurred in the ministry of Jesus should have been made into a resurrection story. On the other hand it is understandable that the resurrection, once believed in, should come to permeate and colour the church's account of the ministry. They saw the ministry of Jesus through eyes opened by the resurrection. In particular the tradition of an appearance to Peter on the Lake of Galilee is retained by placing it in the ministry, for Luke has no place in his Gospel for Galilean appearances.

In the tradition, therefore, the appearance took place while Peter was fishing, and it involved a miraculous catch of fish at the command of one whom Peter came to recognise as the risen Lord. Peter jumped from the boat to meet him and in the ensuing dialogue Peter acknowledged his sin and was restored to favour. Peter then received a commission that gave him pre-eminent authority in the community. John 21 preserves this story faithfully, with admixtures of another appearance story involving a meal. It could also be that the shepherd imagery of John 21 and the rock foundation imagery of Matthew 16, 18 are fragments of a once longer dialogue about the rehabilitation, and giving of authority to Peter. For the imagery of shepherding in the Old Testament does not just refer to care but to authority.

The tradition summarised in the preceding paragraph is early and is reflected in all the Gospels. From a psychological point of view the story makes sense. Peter, confused and frightened after his betrayal of Christ and the crucifixion, returned to his home and old occupation as quickly as he could. There he encountered the risen Lord in a way that spoke to his need and condition. For he was assured by the risen Lord that he was not only taken back into discipleship but given authority for pastoring the infant church.

The Appearance to the Twelve

In the earliest tradition about the resurrection of Christ, transmitted by Paul, an appearance 'to the twelve' is mentioned immediately after the appearance to Peter. When and where did this appearance take place? The Gospel narratives offer rather different accounts. Mark's Gospel points to an appearance in Galilee. The angel tells Mary Magdalene, 'But go, tell his disciples and Peter that he is going before you to Galilee; there you will see him, as he told you.' Matthew's Gospel, which contains only one resurrection appearance, places it in Galilee. On 'the mountain to which Jesus had directed them' the risen Lord appears to the eleven disciples and commissions them to go out into the world. This tradition of a Galilean appearance is also retained in John 21, where Jesus appears by the side of the Lake and offers seven disciples bread and fish.

On the other hand Luke 24, 36–43 recounts how the risen Lord appeared to his disciples in Jerusalem and had a meal with them. Similarly John 20, 19–29 recounts an appearance in Jerusalem, first to the disciples without Thomas and then to Thomas with the other disciples also present. The Markan appendix, Mark 16, 9–19, also retains this tradition.

The traditional way of reconciling these two traditions is to say that Jesus appeared to his disciples in Jerusalem in the days immediately following the resurrection and then sometime later appeared to them in Galilee. But this way of harmonising the two traditions derives from John's Gospel and it is generally agreed by New Testament scholars that John 21, which preserves the Galilean appearance, was written by a different hand from the rest of the Gospel and to him is due such connecting lines as, 'This was now the third time that Jesus was revealed to his disciples'. If this attempt at combining the two traditions is left aside the matter looks very different. For the stories of an appearance in Jerusalem nowhere suggest that there will be further appearances in Galilee and the ones in Galilee nowhere suggest that there have been previous encounters with the risen Lord in Jerusalem. John 20, for example, leads up to the climax of Thomas's confession, 'My Lord and my God'. Luke ends with the risen Lord leading his disciples out to Bethany, blessing them and then parting from them in a way which seems reminiscent of the Ascension story.

The Galilean stories also seem complete in themselves and betray no sign of an earlier appearance in Jerusalem. The disciples are fearful, and some are doubtful, which would hardly be the case if these appearances were just confirmations of what they already knew, that God had raised Christ Jesus. Moreover, as mentioned, Mark's Gospel leads up to an appearance in Galilee with no suggestion that there would be an encounter in Jerusalem first.

It is likely therefore that there was one appearance to the twelve, the memory of which was preserved in somewhat different ways in different communities. The basic elements in this account were:
1) A situation is described in which Jesus' followers are bereft of him.
2) The appearance of Jesus.
3) His greeting to his followers.
4) Their recognition of him.
5) His word of command or commission.

In contrast to the account of the passion it was not obviously necessary for the appearances of the risen Lord to be preserved in a connected narrative.

The passion needed a connected account of what happened from the Last Supper to the burial. But there was no obvious need for a sequential narrative of the resurrection appearances and different communities preserved different memories. Behind these diverse memories was the tradition of an appearance to 'the twelve'. As we have these accounts in the Gospels the particular commission or command which the risen Lord gives his disciples reflects the outlook and theology of the Gospel writer. In Matthew for example the disciples are told to make disciples of all nations, 'baptising them in the name of the Father and of the Son and of the Holy Spirit'. In Luke the risen Lord expounds the scriptures to them and promises them the Holy Spirit. In John 20 the disciples are authorised to forgive sins. This of course raises the question whether the risen Lord communicated with his followers in words. It is closely linked to the other question of in what sense they 'saw' him. Fuller discussion of these questions must wait but we cannot rule out the possibility that in some sense they both 'saw' and 'heard' him speak words to them. Nevertheless, it is possible that a basic commissioning of the disciples, in which the glorified Lord gave his spirit to them and sent them out to proclaim that the Kingdom of God has broken into the world, was gradually unfolded by the disciples as they penetrated the implications of this message. They came, rightly, to see that this involved bearing witness, baptising and forgiving.

It is likely that this appearance to 'the twelve' took place in Galilee, the tradition preserved by Mark, Matthew and John 21. It is easy to understand how the disciples, confused and frightened as a result of the events surrounding the crucifixion should return to their homes and previous occupations (at least some of them came from Galilee). There, by the Lake, the risen Lord met them, strengthened them and commissioned them. On the hypothesis that the risen Lord first encountered his disciples in Jerusalem it is impossible to understand how, once charged with the mission of the risen Lord they should then return to their former occupations. On the other hand if the appearance to the disciples took place in Galilee it is easy to understand why they should have returned to Jerusalem at a later point for the feast of Pentecost and there have received dramatic confirmation of the presence of the Spirit.

There is, however, a possible alternative. An appearance to a group of the disciples in Galilee and to another group who remained in Jerusalem. As already indicated 'the twelve' is a technical term with heavy theological overtones. It signifies the successors to the twelve tribes of Israel, the new twelve who will be in authority in the church, the new Israel, who will judge the world. It became increasingly important to the church that 'the twelve' were witnesses to the resurrection and that they stand as a symbol of the unity of the church in its earliest days. But there were in fact only eleven, Judas having defected. At the first appearance to the assembled group in Jerusalem in John 20, Thomas being absent, there were only 10. In John 21, there are 7 disciples. So it is possible that the disciples did not remain together as a group in the aftermath of the crucifixion. Indeed it seems on *a priori* grounds of general psychology that they did not. It could be that the majority fled to Galilee and a few stayed in Jerusalem. Later at Pentecost they joined together again – and very early the tradition of a twelve who were together all the time circulated.

If we have to choose between an appearance to the twelve in Galilee and an appearance to them in Jerusalem, the former is by far the stronger claimant, for reasons already given. But it is possible that the disciples split up, with at least seven going to Galilee where they then encountered the risen Lord. Meanwhile in Jerusalem the few who remained behind also knew his risen presence, an experience which gave rise to the Jerusalem stories, including that of the appearance of the risen Lord to two disciples on the road to Emmaus. At Pentecost they came together again, when the Galilee group came down for the festival in order to begin to carry out the Lord's mission. From Pentecost it was only natural to think of the twelve as having acted together as a group from the first days.

The Appearance to Mary Magdalene

John 20, 11–18 records an appearance to Mary Magdalene. Mary is weeping outside the tomb. Some angels appear and ask her why she is weeping. She replies that it is because someone has taken away her Lord. She then saw Jesus but did not recognise him, supposing him to be the gardener. In the subsequent dialogue, in which she does recognise him, she is told not to hold him but to go and tell the disciples that he is ascending to their God and Father.

John's Gospel does not stand alone in recording an appearance to Mary Magdalene. The Markan Appendix (Mark 16, 9–19) records:

> Now when he rose early on the first day of the week, he appeared first to Mary Magdalene, from whom he had cast out seven demons. She went and told those who had been with him . . .

Although some believe that this Markan Appendix is simply a summary of the evidence in Matthew, Luke and John compiled by some unknown hand to fill the gap at the end of Mark's Gospel, other scholars have argued strongly that we have here a tradition that is independent of the other Gospels.

Matthew also records an appearance to Mary Magdalene. As Mary is running from the tomb to tell the disciples that she and the other Mary have discovered the tomb empty:

> Behold, Jesus met them and said, 'Hail.' And they came up and took hold of his feet and worshipped him. Then Jesus said to them, 'Do not be afraid; go and tell my brethren to go to Galilee, and there they will see me'.

This passage, it has also been argued, was also originally an independent narrative. It fits awkwardly into the present context. In other words, it was not invented by

Matthew. He knew the story and tried to fit it in even though it somewhat breaks up the sequence of his narrative.

We have therefore three independent testimonies to an appearance to Mary Magdalene. And whilst it is true that the written sources that now contain them – John, Matthew and the Markan Appendix – are late, that is, they probably date from the last decade of the first century, the oral tradition on which they are based is earlier. It seems that there was an original story which described Mary as disconsolate because she thought the body had been taken away. Jesus appeared to her and as he spoke she recognised him. He directed her to go and tell his brothers, which she did. It is quite possible also that the original form of the story gave an indication of place and time, early on Easter morning by the tomb, and contained a reference to Mary seizing the feet of Jesus, which is hinted at in John's, 'Do not hold me'.

Another significant fact is that whenever Mary Magdalene is mentioned in company with other women, she is mentioned first. This may also reflect a tradition that she encountered the risen Lord. There yet remains the disconcerting fact that in the list of appearances cited by Paul in 1 Corinthians 15, there is no mention of Jesus being seen by Mary Magdalene. This tradition, scholars are agreed, is our earliest evidence. Yet in the context of the time it is perhaps not so strange. As already mentioned the evidence of a woman would not have been regarded as reliable, in an official sense, and a woman could not be an apostle: the relationship between being a witness to the resurrection and apostleship being very close.

Mary could not, because of her sex, be an apostle. But the mark of an apostle was the ability to witness to the resurrection, a criterion Mary fulfilled. St Paul is very concerned to place himself in this category but could not include Mary because of her sex. There was therefore a motive not to say anything about Mary Magdalene or the other women.

The account of an appearance to Mary Magdalene in John's Gospel reflects some major theological themes, a few shared by other writers and others distinctively Johannine. First, there is a prolonged period before Mary recognises Jesus. At first she thinks he is the gardener. The theological message behind this may be to stress that the resurrection body of Jesus was a transfigured body, not the same as his earthly body. It is parallel to Paul's teaching that we are changed and that we have a spiritual body. This theme is common to the resurrection narratives in all the Gospels. Mark 16, 12, part of the Markan Appendix, puts it succinctly: 'After this he appeared in *another form* to two of them as they were walking into the country'. Secondly, Mary knows Jesus when he calls her by name. Sight alone does not lead to faith. She saw Jesus but did not recognise him. But when his word addresses her she does. Similarly, in the Emmaus story, the two disciples see and walk with Jesus without recognising him. It is when they hear him expounding the scriptures and when he breaks bread with them that they know who he is. In John, hearing the voice of the Lord, and in particular being called by name, has a profound importance. The true shepherd enters by the door, 'the sheep hear his voice, and he calls his own sheep by name and leads them out'.

There is, thirdly, the dialogue between Mary and the risen Lord. Mary, thinking he is the gardener, asks him to tell her where the body is.

Jesus said to her, 'Mary'. She turned and said to him in Hebrew, 'Rabboni!' (which means Teacher). Jesus said to her, 'Do not hold me, for I have not yet ascended to the Father; but go to my brethren and say to them, I am ascending to my Father and your Father, to my God and your God.' (John 20, 16–17)

This famous scene which has given birth to so many superb 'Noli me Tangere' paintings has been interpreted very variously, sometimes absurdly and often unconvincingly. The clue to what may be the true interpretation of this puzzling passage is in such texts as John 14, 18–19, where Jesus promises his followers that he will not leave them desolate but that he will return and because he lives they will live also; and John 16, 22 where Jesus promises his friends they will see him and he will give them a joy that no one will take from them. John's Gospel thinks in terms of Jesus being glorified through his whole life and death. This life and death is at the same time a 'going to' the Father. As a result of this going to the Father and glorification the Spirit will come to his followers and they will have, through this Spirit, a new, intimate and unbreakable union with him. When Jesus says to Mary, 'Do not hold me, for I have not yet ascended', he is telling her that she cannot *yet* have his enduring presence through the Spirit. The stress is not on 'Do not hold me' but 'Do not hold me *yet*'. In addressing Jesus as Rabboni, a caritative term meaning something like 'My dear Rabbi', Mary uses a modest title that indicates it is still possible to follow Jesus in the old way as a teacher. But she has to grow from this understanding into one which knows his enduring presence through the spirit.

There is also a point worth noting about the affirmation, 'My father and your father, to my God and your God'. The purpose of this is not to emphasise the distinction between the God and Father of Jesus and the God and Father of the disciples but to stress that they are one. Through the spirit Jesus and his followers have become brethren: 'go to my brethren'. The God and Father of Jesus has become their God and Father.

The presence of such theological themes raises the question of how much real history lies behind the incidents in which they occur. The general question is considered in chapter five. It is argued there that all historical writing involves a perspective of some kind and every writer in the New Testament, not just John, has a particular perspective but that this does not mean that there is no basis in fact. Every incident has to be treated individually. The particular question raised at this point is a very wide one; the reliability, from a historical point of view, of John's traditions. More particularly there is the question of the source of the Mary Magdalene incident.

There are some, albeit a minority, of reputable New Testament scholars who accept the early tradition that John's Gospel was written by the Apostle John, one of the sons of Zebedee, himself. He wrote it in great old age at Ephesus. There is another early tradition that Mary Magdalene went with John to Ephesus. It is possible, therefore, that the account of Christ's appearance to Mary Magdalene goes back through John to Mary herself. The little we know of Mary Magdalene from the Fourth Gospel suggests an intimacy. For, standing by the cross were, amongst others, Mary the mother of Jesus, Mary Magdalene and 'the disciple whom he loved.' Jesus said to his mother:

'Woman, behold your son!' Then he said to
the disciple, 'Behold your mother!' And from that
hour the disciple took her to his own home.
(John 19, 26–7)

Mary the mother of Jesus was taken into the home of
John. Mary Magdalene was part of that intimate group.
It is quite possible that behind John's account lies what
Mary Magdalene herself told him. For although the
dialogue between Mary and the risen Lord reflects John's
theology, the truth it communicates is one that would fit
very well with Mary's own experience. She had been an
intimate follower of Jesus in his earthly mission. She had
ministered to his needs and perhaps provided for his
wherewithal. She had particular reason for gratitude, in
that she had been cured of some terrible spiritual
ailment. After the resurrection, if she was going to
remain a follower of Jesus at all, the whole nature of that
following had to be recast. It could no longer be a
physical following about the country of one she addressed
as 'Rabbi'. It had to be non-physical; a relationship with
a non-material spiritual presence. Yet this spiritual
presence she discovered did not mean less in the way of
intimacy but more. This was a presence that brought a
peace and a joy that nothing could destroy. Furthermore,
this presence brought her into a new intimate relationship
with all other followers of the risen Lord; they were
brethren, members of one close family under the one
God and Father, who was as much their God and Father
as he was that of Jesus. It is certain that this fundamental
shift took place in the mind of Mary Magdalene – for she
could not have continued to be a follower unless it had
taken place. Nor is there any real reason to doubt that it
began in an experienced encounter with the risen Lord

shortly after her discovery of the empty tomb. Mary, seeing the one she believed might be the Lord, really did want to hold on to him physically; what is more natural? She took hold of his feet, as the tradition preserved in Matthew puts it. She learns through the risen Christ that there will indeed be an unbroken intimate communion, but that this will be as a result of the Spirit, the Spirit that comes from his risen, ascended and glorified presence. In making this theme explicit in terms of his own language and theology the author of John is not departing from what is likely to have occurred in the mind of Mary Magdalene herself.

The Appearance to Paul

In his evidence for the resurrection, which Paul cites in 1 Corinthians 15, he writes, 'Last of all, as to one untimely born, he appeared also to me.' It is quite clear from this passage that Paul thinks of the appearance of the risen Lord to him as being in the same category as the appearance to Peter, the twelve and others. How does this square with Luke's account? For according to Luke the risen Lord appeared in a unique way to some of his followers during the 40 days after the resurrection. He then ascended into heaven, the Spirit came at Pentecost and thereafter his presence was known in a different, less tangible manner. Paul's conversion took place between three and six years after the death of Jesus. So his encounter on the road to Damascus took place a long time after the 40 days. Luke has three very dramatic accounts of this conversion and though he makes it clear that Paul was indeed apprehended by the risen Lord, in Luke's understanding, Paul did not see Jesus in the same way that the disciples did on the road to Emmaus, or the apostles as they ate with him. Paul's experience is much more akin to a vision; it is in part private to him. It seems therefore that Paul and Luke's understanding of what Paul experienced cannot be totally reconciled. In view of Luke's over neat theological schema, with such importance placed on the symbolic number 40, (40 years in the wilderness, 40 days in the desert etc) Paul's understanding of the matter is to be preferred. The risen Lord appeared to him in the same manner that he had appeared to the apostles before him.

Paul uses the Greek word *ophthe* to say what happened. This is the passive of the verb 'to see' but with the dative, as in this case, is usually translated 'He appeared'. What kind of appearing or seeing is this? In the Old Testament the word is sometimes used for seeing spiritual realities, like angels; but of course for those writers this seeing was understood to be as real, as tangible as seeing apples or oranges. Elsewhere, however, where Paul writes about his experience he uses language susceptible of less tangible interpretation. Writing to the Galatians about how he had once been a persecutor of the Church Paul says that God 'was pleased to reveal his Son to me'.

According to Luke (in the account, Acts 9, 1–9[3]), Paul experienced a blinding light and heard a voice. Those who were with him heard the voice but saw no one. As Paul approached Damascus:

> suddenly a light from heaven flashed about him. And he fell to the ground and heard a voice saying to him, 'Saul, Saul, why do you persecute me?' And he said, 'Who are you, Lord?' And he said, 'I am Jesus, whom you are persecuting; but rise and enter the city, and you will be told what you are to do.' The men who were travelling with him stood speechless, hearing the voice but seeing no one.

Some have suggested that Paul saw only the light, he did not see Jesus himself. Yet elsewhere Paul does write of seeing: 'Have I not seen Jesus our Lord?'

Two points are worth noting about Paul's experience. First, the fierceness of it. The account in Acts 9 continues:

> Saul arose from the ground; and when his eyes were opened, he could see nothing; so that they led him by the hand and brought him to Damascus. And for three days he was without sight, and neither ate nor drank.

Paul, as we know, was zealous for the Jewish law. So strongly did he feel about it that he was prepared to kill those who deviated from it. He was amongst those who watched and approved of the stoning to death of Stephen. He himself took the initiative in rounding up Christians in Damascus. He had no doubt that Jesus was a criminal and blasphemer, an enemy of God whose followers needed to be hunted down and routed out in the name of God. This fanatical fierceness against the followers of Jesus came, on the Damascus road, face to face with Jesus himself: with Jesus in and through his followers, it is worth noting. The words he heard were, 'I am Jesus whom you are persecuting'. It was the followers of Jesus whom Paul was actively persecuting. This encounter with the risen Lord demanded a total reversal of what he believed. Jesus was not God's enemy but his chosen one. Not a blasphemer but God's son. It is hardly surprising that the total change demanded should have struck Paul blind for three days and made him incapable of taking food or drink.

Secondly, however, this reversal as a result of meeting the risen Lord on the road to Damascus was not unrelated to Paul's whole religious quest. It is a cliché of psychology that we are most fierce in opposition to those who in some way trouble us and get a foothold inside us. Clearly Jesus and what he stood for had got right under Paul's skin; enough under his skin to make him want to wipe his followers off the face of the earth. For what Jesus stood for was a direct threat to all that Paul had come to believe. In Paul's letter to the Romans and his other writings we get some insight into why, under the surface, what Jesus stood for was such a threat to the old Saul. For Saul believed that the Torah was the revealed will of God and obedience to it the way of salvation. But could the Torah bring about that fundamental change of heart from which true love springs? Jesus, on the other hand, offered not the Torah but the presence of the kingdom, God's rule on earth; and his followers claimed that this kingdom was present in Jesus himself. They offered not the Torah but mystical union with the risen Jesus as the way to salvation. Did this mystical union bring about that fundamental change of heart from which genuine love could spring? Some such thoughts and feelings may have been going through his mind for some years before that decisive encounter on the road to Damascus.

4

Forms of Christ's Presence in the World

'I am with you always'

Some people claim to have encountered the risen
Christ in a way which is completely self-authenticating.
They do not simply talk about God, or the Holy
Spirit, but Christ. They claim to have experienced not
an undifferentiated spiritual presence but a divine
presence identical with Jesus of Nazareth. For example,
Cuthbert Bardsley, the former Bishop of Coventry, has
written:

> When my youngest sister died at the age of twenty-
> six I was inconsolable. After my father's death, she
> had been a close companion, gay and vital.
> Suddenly, she was stricken. Within days she was
> dead. Before the funeral, I went into a village
> church to mourn, and be alone. A long time I sat
> there, deeply distressed. And then – quite suddenly
> and unemotionally, I knew that he was there,
> comforting and encouraging. There took place in
> that church in fact, an encounter with the risen
> Lord which has often put me in mind of the
> experience of Mary Magdalen in the garden. I

knew that my Redeemer lived, and because of that, my sister lived.[4]

Some people who claim to have had this experience (not Cuthbert Bardsley) imply that such an encounter is the essential distinguishing mark of a true Christian. But such an implication is quite unwarranted. Very many Christians, of unimpeachable Evangelical credentials, would claim no such experience. For example, one of the greatest of the Evangelical preachers of the 19th century, Dr John Hunter, in discussing the phrase 'communion with the living Christ' and the danger that it should become the symbol of a party wrote:

> When I was a lad of 10 I was deeply moved by the religious revival that swept the North of Scotland and Ireland in 1859 and 1860. I still have in me I think the best spiritual results of those early experiences and still later 'Evangelical' experiences; but not at any time of my life have I been conscious of holding any communion with the living Christ as an experience separate and distinct from communion with the living God. In my most 'evangelical' days I could never pray to Christ, only to the Father in the name of Christ, as I do today. It also seems to me that the consciousness of sonship to God – the filial consciousness – and not the 'direct communication of the soul with the saviour' is the distinctive note of the Christian experience.[5]

Yet however we experience the fact and however we talk about it the whole of the New Testament reflects the experience that the living Christ is present in his church. Not, to be sure, in exactly the same way that he was present to, and known by, the apostles in the period after the first Easter. Paul, in 1 Corinthians 15, clearly implies that after his own experience on the Damascus Road there have been no comparable encounters either to him or to any of the other apostles. 'Last of all, as to one untimely born, he appeared also to me.' The Fourth Gospel, which was perhaps written when the generation of first witnesses was dying out, is at pains to point out that although later Christians do not 'see' Christ in the way that the first Christians did, their experience is no less valid. According to the fourth evangelist Jesus said to Thomas, 'Have you believed because you have seen me? Blessed are those who have not seen and yet believe.'

St Matthew's Gospel leads up to the great climax on a mountain in Galilee where the risen, exalted Lord commissions the eleven disciples. He tells them to make disciples of all nations, baptising them in the name of the Trinity, teaching them to be obedient to what Christ has taught them and ending with the words: 'and lo, I am with you always, to the close of the age'. Christ promises his presence with his followers but not, presumably in the way he was present with the eleven on the mountain or with Mary Magdalene in Jerusalem where she took hold of his feet. The closing affirmation in Matthew recalls two earlier statements in the Gospel. Matthew 1, 23 says that the child that is to be born 'shall be called Emmanuel (which means, God with us)'. In the earthly ministry of Jesus God is with us and after his crucifixion, resurrection and exaltation he remains with us. Matthew 18, 20 says: 'For where two or three are gathered in my name, there am I in the midst of them'. According to Jewish tradition, where two or three sat with the Torah between them the Shekinah, or divine presence, was with them. But for the early church Jesus had replaced the Torah as the revelation of God's will for them. Where two or three gathered in his name the divine presence is with them. There is in fact surprisingly little emphasis in Matthew on appearances of the risen Lord. What matters to him, writing about 50 years after the crucifixion, is the mission of the church and obedience to Christ's teaching. In this obedience and mission the divine presence, made known in Jesus, remains with his followers. But in what form is he present and how can he be known?

Through the Scriptures

According to Luke two disciples were walking to Emmaus on the first Easter when a stranger joined them and the disciples began to tell him what had happened recently:

> And he said to them, 'O foolish men, and slow of heart to believe all that the prophets have spoken! Was it not necessary that the Christ should suffer these things and enter into his glory?' And beginning with Moses and all the prophets, he interpreted to them in all the scriptures the things concerning himself. (Luke 24, 25–27)

When they had recognised that this stranger was the risen Christ the two disciples said to one another, 'Did not our hearts burn within us while he talked to us on the road, while he opened to us the scriptures?' As the two disciples got back to Jerusalem and were telling the others about their experience Christ came amongst them. He told them everything written about him in the law of Moses had to be fulfilled:

> Then he opened their minds to understand the scriptures, and said to them, 'Thus it is written, that the Christ should suffer and on the third day rise from the dead . . .'

Whatever historical basis there may be to the encounter on the road to Emmaus it is clear that the form of the story as we have it at the moment reflects the experience not just of two disciples but of the church as a whole, in knowing Christ through the scriptures.

It is basic to the Bible that God chose the people of Israel to reveal his mind and will, not only to them but to the world as a whole. This revealing was a long, cumulative, painful process, with many setbacks. But at its heart was a relationship between the God who promised to be faithful and his people who sought to be obedient. In this struggle God revealed, and his people grasped, something of his purpose. Sometimes certain named people played an inspired role. Sometimes it was anonymous interpreters of these key people, schools of thought that they set in motion. The result was that a body of words grew up, stories, laws, sayings, myths, prophecies and so on, which recorded successive moments in the relationship and what was disclosed, or grasped, as a result of them. These interpretations and reinterpretations of the glorious and painful struggle of the people of Israel with their God built up a picture of his will and purpose. After the crucifixion the bewildered disciples of Christ looked to this body of words to see if it could help make sense of what had happened. With great excitement they found that it did : 'Did not our hearts burn within us . . .' As they read the scriptures and reflected on their experience in the light of them, it seemed that Christ himself was opening their minds to understand.

Later a body of Christian words grew up; words that reflected the life of the new church, letters written by Paul, collections of stories of what Jesus did, collections of sayings of what he said. After a long process of sifting, these were collected and began to constitute what we call the New Testament. And it has been the conviction of Christians down the ages that as they reflected on their experience in the light of these words, as the first disciples reflected on their experience in the light of what later came to be called the Old Testament, the Holy Spirit opened their minds and revealed to them the mind of Christ.

God chose to reveal himself in the midst of the confusion and betrayals of a human community. He did not stay aloof and apart, sending occasional thunderbolts and dictates down from on high. He immersed himself in the life of his people. Words resulted from this immersion and those words remain. Like the tidemark they show where God has been. But the sea is still with us. Christ is still present with his people. And he continues to make himself known through words – through the words of scripture and preaching and prayer. As Bonhoeffer has written:

> In our meditation we ponder the chosen text on the strength of the promise that is has something utterly personal to say to us for this day and for our Christian life, that it is not only God's Word for the Church, but also God's Word for us individually. We expose ourselves to the specific word until it addresses us personally. And when we do this, we are doing no more than the simplest, untutored Christian does every day; we read God's Word as God's Word for us.
>
> We do not ask what this text has to say to other people. For the preacher this means that he will not ask how he is going to preach or teach on this text, but what it is saying quite directly to him. It is true

that to do this we must first have understood the content of the verse, but here we are not expounding it or preparing a sermon or conducting Bible study of any kind; we are rather waiting for God's Word to us. It is not a vacuous waiting, but a waiting on the basis of a clear promise. Often we are so burdened and overwhelmed with other thoughts, images and concerns that it may take a long time before God's Word has swept all else aside and come through. But it will surely come, just as surely as God himself has come to men and will come again. This is the very reason why we begin our meditation with the prayer that God may send his Holy Spirit to us through his Word and reveal his Word to us and enlighten us.[6]

Christ is always present with his people but words are a special vehicle for making that presence known. The Divine Word speaks to us in and through the words of that community of faith in which he has chosen to dwell in a special way. An analogy, or rather, two analogies can make the point. A country has been occupied by enemy forces and the king has had to flee into exile. From exile he plans to overthrow the enemy and with that end in view sends messengers to loyal followers in his own country. Through these messages the followers keep their hopes alive; through pondering the words of the king they divine his plans. It is true they do not see the king nor can they ever prove that the words are his, for his words come through intermediaries. But through listening to the words of the intermediaries, the loyal followers believe they can discern the mind of the king behind them and make out his purpose. The words of the messengers are carriers of the words of the sovereign and these words disclose the sovereign's mind.

This analogy, like all analogies, breaks down. For it deals with a situation in which the king is absent. The Christian church claims that Christ, though invisible, is present spiritually. So another analogy is needed. A man calls on his brother, whom he has not seen for twenty years. During that time the brother has gone blind. But as soon as the returning brother speaks there is instant recognition. The brother is physically present, standing at the front door. But as he cannot be seen it is words that bring the recognition of his presence. This analogy too, of course, breaks down. For in this picture the blind man can actually hear the words of his returning brother. The church, however, cannot hear the words of God. They come to us through human words. So, extending this second analogy we imagine that the brother has gone not only blind but deaf. He cannot hear the words. Yet there is a friend present who can type the words on to a braille typewriter. The deaf and blind brother can read braille and through this means he has access to the words and mind of his returning brother. Even this extended analogy fails in the end. But the main point has perhaps been made. Human words can convey the divine word and this divine word is the Christ who is present with his disciples.

Two clarifying points need to be made. First, although all human words, like every aspect of the created order, can reveal to us something of God, the above account assumes that the words of Scripture are in a special sense revelatory. This stems from the fact that Israel is a uniquely chosen people and Christ is the eternal Son of God incarnate. The words that resulted from this unique disclosure have a special place in making known in every age the presence of the eternal word who took flesh and died and rose again.

Secondly, this emphasis on the words of the Bible having a special place in conveying to us the reality of Christ is in no way to be confused with what is called a fundamentalist or literalist approach to the Bible. Fundamentalism is in fact an unbiblical form of Christianity. As Professor James Barr has written:

> Fundamentalism is the imposition upon the Bible of a particular tradition of human religion, and the use of the Bible as an instrument of power to secure the success and influence of that form of religion. Again and again fundamentalist religion contradicts the realities of the Bible.[7]

It is not necessary to be a fundamentalist to believe that Christ speaks to us in and through the words of scripture. It is possible to use all the tools of modern Biblical scholarship and still to look in the scriptures for the mind of Christ and the word of God.

In the Eucharist

In the Emmaus story the two disciples did not recognise the stranger who walked with them until the meal they shared in the evening:

> When he was at table with them, he took the bread and blessed, and broke it, and gave it to them. And their eyes were opened and they recognised him; and he vanished out of their sight. (Luke 24, 30–31)

Then, after they had returned and told the other disciples, the risen Christ again stood amongst them. They gave him a piece of broiled fish and he took it and ate before them. Similarly in John 21, as was mentioned earlier, the risen Christ shares a meal with his disciples. When the disciples came in from fishing they see a charcoal fire with fish lying on it and bread:

> Jesus said to them, 'Come and have breakfast.' Now none of the disciples dared asked him, 'Who are you?' They knew it was the Lord. Jesus came and took the bread and gave it to them, and so with the fish. (John 21, 12–13)

As is well known, there is in John's Gospel no account of the Last Supper. However, chapter 6, after recounting the feeding of the five thousand, is given over to a discourse on the bread of life:

> Jesus said to them, 'I am the bread of life . . . I am the living bread which came down from heaven; if anyone eats of this bread, he will live for ever . . . Truly, truly I say to you, unless you eat the flesh of the Son of Man and drink his blood, you have no life in you; he who eats my flesh and drinks my blood has eternal life . . . As the living Father sent me, and I live because of the father, so he who eats me will live because of me . . .'

It is difficult to escape the conclusion that this profound and disturbing discourse reflects the Church's experience of the risen Christ in the Eucharist.

We know from Paul and from what Luke records in Acts that from the first days of the church it was the custom for Christians to meet together for a common meal after the pattern of the Last Supper. In this meal, as is clear from the references already quoted, they knew the risen Lord to be present in a specially intimate way. So it has been down the ages. Whatever disputes there have been between the churches over how Christ is present no denomination has believed in the real absence of Christ in the Eucharist. All churches meet in response to what they believe to be his command, 'Do this in remembrance of me', and in partaking of the bread believe they are receiving the bread of life, Christ himself.

Christ is present with his people in a variety of ways. He is present as the ground of our being, the fount from whom and through whom creation flows. He is present in the secret places of our heart as our true self, the soul of our soul. He is more present the more we allow him to permeate our lives, so that he is more in a good person than a bad one, more in a saint than a sinner. It has been the experience of the church from the earliest days that he is specially present in the community. 'Where two or three are gathered together in my name.' For Christianity is concerned not only with the maturing of the individual life but of the growth into Christ of the whole community, of people in their relationships with one another. Meals have always played a special part in human life. They have rarely been regarded simply as a means of taking nourishment on board. The social element has always been strong. A group of friends or a family sitting down for a meal together is a focus of what human life should be. So it is not surprising that the Jews thought of the Kingdom of God as a heavenly banquet and that this image should have been dominant in the mind of Christ himself. It is not surprising that in his historical ministry Christ should have shared intimate meals with his disciples or that he should have had one last meal with them; or in the light of this that the early church should have continued to meet for a meal in his name, and that the church should have continued to do so down the ages. Although in the past there have been some sad divisions over the Eucharist, one of the encouraging features is the way these old disagreements are now being overcome. For example, the Anglican Roman Catholic International Commission (ARCIC) statement on the Eucharist had this to say about Christ's presence in the Eucharist:

> Christ is present and active, in various ways, in the entire eucharistic celebration. It is the same Lord who through the proclaimed word invites his people to his table, who through his minister presides at that table, and gives himself sacramentally in the body and blood of his paschal sacrifice. It is the Lord present at the right hand of the Father, and therefore transcending the sacramental order, who thus offers to his Church, in the eucharistic signs, the special gift of himself.[8]

Resurrection Life out of Suffering

Paul claimed to have been grasped by the risen Lord on the road to Damascus. He also experienced an overwhelming mystical experience. Apart from these two experiences however, Paul writes about communion with the risen Christ in terms of mystical incorporation. His most distinctive phrase for Christians is that they are 'the body of Christ'. The head of the body has broken the barriers of time and space to be with God in heaven: but his body remains on earth. Christians are limbs or members of this body. No less important is Paul's understanding of Christians as people who are 'In Christ'. A spatial metaphor is used to indicate that we are now joined to and part of Christ himself.

One of the most profound and important ways in which Paul conceives of this union however, is through suffering. Paul, who suffered much, thinks of his suffering as a sharing in the suffering of Christ. But out of this suffering comes resurrection life. He wrote to the Corinthians:

> always carrying in the body the death of Jesus, so that the life of Jesus may also be manifested in our bodies. For while we live we are always being given up to death for Jesus' sake, so that the life of Jesus may be manifested in our mortal flesh. So death is at work in us, but life in you. (2 Corinthians 4, 10–12)

To another church Paul wrote:

> For his sake I have suffered the loss of all things, and count them as refuse that I may gain Christ and be found in him . . . that I may know him and the power of his resurrection, and may share his sufferings, becoming like him in his death, that if possible I may attain the resurrection from the dead. (Philippians 3, 8–11)

This theme is particularly strong in the Orthodox Church. There resurrection as a present reality is much more prominent than it has tended to be in the Western churches. The role of suffering and suffering love has been seen as charged with possibilities for the emergence of resurrection life. In Dostoevsky's novel *Crime and Punishment* a strange creature called Raskolnikov murders two old ladies for no apparent motive. Raskolnikov is befriended by Sonia, a saintly loving girl, who has been forced into prostitution by the destitution of her family. The turning point of Raskolnikov's life comes when

Sonia reads him the account of the raising of Lazarus, focusing in particular on the phrases, 'I am the resurrection and the life' and 'Whosoever liveth and believeth in me shall never die'. Raskolnikov is eventually sent to Siberia where Sonia follows him. The book ends on a note of hope. Through Sonia's love and suffering Raskolnikov has been raised from spiritual death. Christ's resurrection life is at work in him through her.

Quite properly the different forms of Christ's presence in the world are intertwined with one another. When he was in prison Oscar Wilde suffered terribly:

> I have lain in prison for nearly two years. Out of my nature has come wild despair; and abandonment to grief that was piteous to look at; terrible and impotent rage; bitterness and scorn; anguish that wept aloud.[9]

Yet in and through this suffering he learnt priceless truths. Sorrow, he found, to be a searching and wise teacher. He was also helped by the Gospels. Every morning after he had cleaned his cell and polished his tins he read a little of the Gospels. Later, when released from prison and before he died Wilde was received into the Roman Catholic church. But it was his time in prison that was decisive. He wrote, 'Once at least in his life each man walks with Christ to Emmaus'.[10]

In the Needs of Others

There is a remarkable parable in Matthew 25. It is the judgement and human beings are separated into two groups. One group has met the needs of others. The other group failed to do so. What both groups did not know at the time was that what they did or failed to do was in relation to Christ. 'Truly I say to you, as you did it to one of the least of these my brethren, you did it to me.'

This passage has challenged Christians in every age. For example, in 1527 when Breslau in Germany was hard hit by the plague Christians wondered if they ought to stay or flee. Martin Luther wrote an open letter to John Hess in which he said:

> I know very well that if Christ himself or his mother were now ill, everybody would be so devoted as to wish to help and serve . . . Everybody would come running. Yet they do not want to hear what he himself says: 'inasmuch as ye have done it unto one of the least of my brethren, ye have done it unto me'. If then you would minister to and wait upon Christ, behold you have a sick neighbour before you. Go to him and minister to him and you will assuredly find Christ in him.[11]

In our own time Mother Teresa of Calcutta has been particularly inspired by this parable. She has written:

> In Holy Communion we have Christ under the appearance of bread. In our work we find him under the appearance of flesh and blood. It is the same Christ. 'I was hungry, I was naked, I was sick, I was homeless.'[12]

Like others she does not always find this easy. But the attempt to serve Christ in the needs of others informs her prayers.

> Dearest Lord, though you hide yourself behind the unattractive disguise of the irritable, the exacting, the unreasonable, may I still recognise you and say: 'Jesus, my patient, how sweet it is to serve you'.[13]

The Nature of the Risen Presence

It was noted at the beginning of this chapter that in Matthew's Gospel there is very little stress on special appearances of the risen Lord to individual disciples. Rather, the Gospel ends on the marvellously affirmative note for Christians in every age, 'I am with you always'. Christ is present with his church in different ways and the experience of his presence is talked about in different ways. But there is continuity between the experience reflected in the New Testament and that of the Church down the ages. Four forms of Christ's presence that the Church has always regarded as precious have been discussed here. Christ's presence through the scriptures, in the Eucharist, through suffering love and in the needs of the needy. But how should we characterise this presence?

The Gospels vary in their understanding of the manner of Christ's risen presence. Luke thinks very physically, so that the risen Lord even eats fish. Those who were with Paul on the Damascus road, however, saw nothing, though they did hear a voice. Yet all the writers indicate that the risen Christ is no longer bound by space and time. He appears and disappears at will; nor is he instantly recognisable. There is discontinuity as well as continuity between his glorified form and his earthly being. It is difficult to find an adequate phrase to describe the reality they are trying to convey. The difficulty is part of the general difficulty of talking about divine realities in human terms. But there is a special difficulty about the resurrection. for not only does it not fit into any other category: the divine and the human are bound up together in a unique way. The phrase chosen here to indicate the nature of the resurrection appearances in the Gospels is 'objective vision'.

Simplistic thinking makes a sharp distinction between subjective and objective. At the extreme of human apprehension this is valid. A person suffering from schizophrenia who sees someone coming towards him with a knife (when in fact there is no one there) is diagnosed as suffering from a delusion. What the person sees occurs only in their own mind. There is nothing outside that mind which corresponds to it. At the other extreme we have Dr Johnson kicking a lump of stone to show that we do not all live in a subjective world of dreams. There is a reality outside the human mind (difficult though it may be to prove in strict logic). But what is that world outside the human mind? What soon becomes apparent is that what we grasp of that world depends very much on a subjective factor. The poet William Blake once wrote:

> What! It will be questioned when the sun rises; do you not see a round disc of fire, somewhat like a guinea? Oh, no, no, I see an innumerable company of the heavenly host crying Holy, Holy, Holy is the Lord God Almighty.[14]

This sense of seeing more than the generality of humankind sees has been shared by a number of people. Some, like Wordsworth and Traherne, associate it particularly with a pure, childhood apprehension of the world, which adults tend to lose:

> How like an Angel came I down!
> How bright are all things here!
> When first amongst his works I did appear
> O how their Glory did me crown!

The world resembled his eternity,
In which my Soul did walk;
And everything that I did see
Did with me talk.[15]

Some of the writers in this tradition put their stress on
the way the world is luminous to the divine: others on
how the world points beyond itself to some transcendent
realm. It is the same experience described from slightly
different points of view. There is a transcendent realm
but for the most part we only know this as it is
manifested in and through the world. The world
therefore becomes sacramental; an outward and visible
reality mediating this spiritual realm to us. The world
becomes diaphanous. It is the world we see but we see it
in the divine light which upholds and permeates it and
without which it would not be. What we see depends
very much on our inward state. 'Blessed are the pure in
heart for they shall see God.' Or as Blake wrote:

If the doors of perception were cleansed everything
would appear to man as it is, infinite. For man has
closed himself up so till he sees all things thro'
narrow chinks of his cavern.[16]

The poet Francis Thompson wrote:

The angels keep their ancient places;
Turn but a stone and start a wing!
'Tis ye, 'tis your estrangéd faces,
That miss the many-splendoured thing.[17]

These angels that Francis Thompson saw – do they exist
as discrete entities? Or are they a poetic way of talking
about the spiritual realm? However the question is

answered, there is a spiritual realm which is known in and through the finite world. But it can only be 'seen' by people in a particular subjective state. The risen Christ is present to us as the spiritual realm is present. His presence is an objective reality but one which requires a particular inward disposition to apprehend.

According to orthodox Christianity Christ is 'of one substance with the Father'. In him the eternal Son of God united himself to human personhood. During the incarnate life this divine core of his being was hidden. Jesus lived a fully human existence. But after the resurrection this divine substance or essence was reunited with the divine realm, from which, in one sense, it had never been separated. The Divine/human Christ was henceforth part of that unbounded realm, coterminous with God himself. All this is indicated in the phrase 'risen, ascended, glorified'. From this glorified realm and state Christ made his reality known to his followers. But he did so in terms which they could know and recognise. He appeared to them as the Jesus of Nazareth they had known and loved. We saw in chapter three that the risen Christ appeared to people in different ways, in terms of their needs, personalities and situation at the time. To Peter he appeared with a message of rehabilitation. To Mary Magdalene with a message that his abiding joyful presence was of a spiritual not a physical kind. To the twelve with a message to bring the message of the Kingdom to all nations. To Paul, that the one he was persecuting was the Son of God.

This is entirely what we should expect. God works individually with individuals. He meets us at our points of need in terms we can grasp. What united those who first saw him, however, was the conviction that they had seen *Jesus*, the one who had once talked and walked with them.

Here we have to face honestly the fact that Christians after Paul's Damascus road experience have not encountered the risen Lord in terms of the physical features of Jesus of Nazareth. They have known a spiritual presence through the scriptures, in the Eucharist, in suffering love and in the needy. The first Christians, however, claimed to have seen Jesus in humanly recognisable form. This is probably best accounted for in terms of memory and psychology. The risen Lord used the ordinary psychological processes of the disciples, including their memories of his earthly form, to make his reality known to them in a vivid manner. All New Testament writers are agreed that the manner of Christ's appearances in the immediate aftermath of the crucifixion differed from that of succeeding generations. Luke accounted for that difference in terms of ascension, glorification and the coming of the spirit. Christ appeared in one mode before the Ascension and another mode after it. There was indeed a difference. But that difference is best accounted for in terms of the closeness of the first followers of Jesus to his human reality, so that, under the spirit, their grasp of him included a 'seeing' and even the possibility of touching. For succeeding generations the 'seeing' is not associated with the earthly form of Jesus.

This is not, it must be emphasised, reducing the resurrection appearances to a subjective phenomenon or hallucination. It must be stressed again that on the view taken here, first the tomb was really empty and the physical body of Jesus transfigured into the stuff of Glory. Secondly, the risen Christ lives for ever, as God lives; as the second person of the Trinity united with human personhood. Thirdly, this risen Christ objectively appeared to Peter, the twelve, Mary Magdalene, Paul and others. But he appeared to them in the form of the earthly Jesus they had seen and heard. To succeeding generations this could not be so, nor would it be right to be so. For now the universal Christ makes himself known to the Chinese in Chinese terms, to Arabs in Arabic terms and so on. He has been raised to a universal contemporaneity and can be known as we lift our hearts in prayer to God.

5

Interpreting the Evidence

Three points have so far been established. First, contrary to some contemporary New Testament scholarship, the discovery of the empty tomb is an early and well authenticated historical tradition. Whatever reason may be suggested for the emptiness of the tomb, and that remains to be discussed, the story that Mary Magdalene and one or two other women arrived at the tomb early on the first Easter and found it disconcertingly empty, is highly likely to be true. Secondly, from shortly after the crucifixion certain people claimed to have 'seen' the risen Lord. He appeared, so it is claimed, to Peter on the Lake of Galilee and to the majority of the twelve, also in Galilee. He appeared to Mary Magdalene by the tomb on the first Easter and perhaps also to a few of the disciples who remained in Jerusalem rather than returning to Galilee. Some years later he appeared also to Paul. He appeared to other people as well (Paul mentions some of them) though these other appearances have not been discussed here. Thirdly, Christians believe that Christ remains with his church in a spiritual way. Four forms of his presence in particular are reflected in Christian experience and these forms have been valued by the church in every age: through the scriptures, in the

Eucharist, through suffering love and in the needs of the needy. In these ways Christ has been known, loved and served.

These three points have been established. But they do not of themselves prove that Christ was raised from the dead. For it is quite possible to give a sceptical interpretation of them. It could be argued that the tomb was found empty because the body of Jesus had been removed by some unknown person. Although there is no obvious culprit, that some human person removed the body is the natural explanation and therefore more likely, so it is argued, to be true than a supernatural one. Then, the tomb having been found empty and the rumour of this having got about, it triggered off a series of hallucinations. In the stunned and confused state of mind of the disciples after the crucifixion the story that the tomb had been found empty, taken with the huge impact Jesus made on their lives when he was with them, set off a series of experiences of his presence. This was eventually formulated into the church's proclamation that God had raised Jesus from the dead. Once this belief became a basic category of Christian thinking, from then on the spiritual experience of church members would inevitably be interpreted in terms of Christ's presence with them. Church members share with all human beings a capacity for spiritual experience but how this is interpreted varies with the conceptual tools that are available. Within the church, with its basic category that Christ had been raised from the dead, it was inevitable and natural that spiritual experience should be understood in terms of Christ's continuing presence.

This sceptical interpretation of the three points has a certain plausibility. How then can a person come to believe the alternative – that Christ was indeed raised and that he is spiritually present in his church?

First there is the point, often made but none the less telling, of the failure of anyone, friend or enemy, actually to produce the body of Jesus. The Christian claim that God had raised Christ Jesus from the dead would have gone down like a punctured balloon if someone sceptical of, or hostile to, the church's message had produced his body. But there was a singular failure to do so. Nor on the other hand did any cult grow up centred on the grave of Jesus. It is a natural instinct for reverence to be paid to the grave of a holy person and for that spot to become a focus of pilgrimage. But this did not happen. The place where Jesus was buried and raised only began to become of note in the fourth century with the discovery of the Holy sites by Helena, the mother of the Emperor Constantine. The enemies of the church did not produce the body of Jesus; no holy site grew up round his grave and there is no shred of evidence that any of his followers stole the body: not only is there no evidence, it is difficult to see what the motivation would be.

None of this proves the claim that it was God who raised Jesus from the dead. Nevertheless, the absence of convincing alternative explanations is a significant fact in the overall picture. Whether a supreme miracle took place depends in significant measure on a person's presuppositions about miracles. It was suggested in the first chapter that for anyone who believes God created the world *ex nihilo*, and who is active within it fulfilling his purpose, such a miracle is certainly possible. But would such a miracle be in keeping with the way God works? Would it not perhaps be immoral to work such a miracle on this occasion and not on others? That, in substance, is the latest charge made by the Bishop of Durham against the traditional interpretation. This must now be considered.

Why a Unique Miracle?

In his speech at the York meeting of the General Synod of the Church of England in July 1986, the Bishop of Durham gave an impassioned defence of his views on the resurrection. In this speech he accused those who believed in the empty tomb of worshipping 'a cultic idol' or 'the very devil'. He accused them of believing in a 'divine laser beam' with which God had brought about the resurrection. His central argument was that people should not believe in a God who worked miracles on some occasions yet stood by and did nothing miraculous to prevent horrors like Auschwitz and Hiroshima. He said:

> We are faced with the claim that God is prepared to work knock-down physical miracles in order to let a select number of people into the secret of his Incarnation, Resurrection and salvation, but he is not prepared to use such methods in order to deliver from Auschwitz, prevent Hiroshima; overcome famine, or bring about a bloodless transformation of apartheid. Such a God is surely a cultic idol. That is to say he is a false and misdeveloped picture of the true and gracious God, drawn up by would-be worshippers, who have gone dangerously astray.

Such a God, he said, 'prefers a few selected worshippers to all the sufferers of the world'. Such a God 'is certainly not worth believing in'.

The Bishop was right to raise moral questions about belief in particular notions of God. The moral case against God, as put for example by Ivan Karakazov or Albert Camus, is the one that needs to be taken more seriously than any other and far more seriously than is habitual with church members. Nevertheless, raising a question, even in as sharp and controversial a form as the Bishop of Durham raises it, does not mean that it is unanswerable. There are several points that can be made.

First, the Bishop's objection applies to his own view of the resurrection as much as the traditional belief in the empty tomb. For on the Bishop's view the true self of Jesus was indeed raised and appeared as a divine spiritual presence to his followers. If this is not a miracle I do not know what is. For the Bishop will rightly have nothing to do with the view that the appearances were purely subjective, a change in attitude by the disciples. Jesus was objectively, though mysteriously and spiritually, present: the same Jesus who had once lived in flesh and blood. This is a miracle for which many of those who were in Auschwitz would have been extremely grateful. If when a family of Jews was about to go into the gas ovens they had had a clear, totally convincing appearance of their dead relatives who had gone into the ovens before them, this would have given them enormous hope and courage. But the vast majority of those who perished in the ovens had no such experience. In other words, God was willing to make the reality of Jesus' living presence known to his disciples but was not willing to perform the same miracle for those in Auschwitz. The question the Bishop raises, and quite rightly raises, applies no less sharply to his own interpretation of the resurrection than to the traditional one.

Secondly, all Christians are agreed that if God does perform miracles he does so only very occasionally and this for good reason. In order for human beings to exist as the rational creatures they are, it is necessary for them to live in a stable, ordered and predictable environment. It is because the law of gravity and the million other natural laws are indeed 'laws', i.e. observed regularities on the basis of which we can make sensible predictions about the future, such as that the sun will rise tomorrow and a ball thrown in the air will fall to earth again, our minds can develop. An Alice in Wonderland world in which nothing stayed the same from one moment to the next and everything changed in an arbitrary manner would perhaps be fun for a few seconds but after that it would make rational human existence impossible. So there is a limit to what God can do without frustrating his overall purpose of creating free rational beings. For every action in the world has ramifications and ripples that affect every other. If God performed a miracle to prevent a car running over a child that ran in front of it, causing the car to stop in 10 feet instead of the normal optimum stopping distance of 20 feet, that would be wonderful for the child. But what about the car behind? And the car behind that? And the coach load of children just behind that? A most enormous pile-up would ensue. This does not mean that God never performs miracles but it does mean there is a limit to what he can do without disrupting the stable and predictable environment in which alone free rational creatures can exist. So, painful though the thought is, it is possible to understand why God does not act in a miraculous way to deliver from Auschwitz. (He is of course ceaselessly active in non-miraculous ways through people willing to co-operate with his purpose of love.)

Given the fact that God normally works his purposes through people who consciously choose to co-operate with his grace and not through miracles, for the reason given above, the question is raised whether he could *ever* act in a miraculous way, and if so why should he do so for one person rather than another?

Thirdly, it is not necessarily unfair to choose one person rather than another. A family have crashed their plane in the middle of the Amazonian jungle. The father decides to take one of his sons and explore a way out, to see if he can reach help. He leaves his other son with his wife, who is hurt. Is it unfair for the Father to choose one son and leave the other behind? Clearly not, for the ultimate purpose is to save the whole family. If Christ is the object of unique action it is not for his sake alone, nor even simply for his followers, but for the whole of humanity. Or take the example of two friends, both badly crippled, who go to Lourdes. One of them is cured and the other is not. But the one who is cured spends the rest of her life caring for the one who remained crippled. And a wonderful relationship built up between them. Given God's overall purpose of creating free rational beings, with the consequence of working miracles only very rarely, it is possible to see how this situation, in which one friend was miraculously healed and the other was not, might both safeguard God's overall purposes and at the same time witness to the way he works through ordinary processes and human co-operation to bring good out of evil.

Fourthly, God has chosen to achieve his purpose in the world not simply by co-operation with his will through the inspiration of the Holy Spirit, but to come amongst us as a human person and win our allegiance at our level, in human terms. So there is, on a Christian view, a unique strand in the world's history. God chooses a people and calls them to a vocation of sonship through which his purpose will be known. This vocation comes to a climax in Jesus, in whom God dwells. After the crucifixion God continues to be with us through his son, in his body the church, its loving fellowship, words of scripture, preaching and Eucharistic fellowship. God works for the salvation of the world not just 'from on high' through his overall providence, nor just 'from below' through the permeation of the Holy Spirit at the root of the world's being but 'in our midst'. God has immersed himself in the stream of human history. In this way he both respects human freedom and acts upon us in a persuasive way through his son. So, on any Christian view, Christ is unique. But his uniqueness exists in order to bring salvation to the whole human race.

The Bishop is therefore quite misleading in saying that the miracle of the resurrection was performed 'to let a select number of people into the secret of his Incarnation, Resurrection and salvation'. The resurrection was performed as part of his purpose of bringing salvation to the whole human race. If that purpose was going to be achieved it was essential that at least a few people should be called into an active sharing in that work. Hence Jesus called some people into intimate friendship with himself. After his resurrection he assured them of his continued presence and commissioned them to continue his work. God works in two modes. He works equally with everyone through his Spirit. He also works within a narrow, but expanding, stream of history which in Christian hope will widen out to include and redeem the whole of humanity.

To sum up the points made in relation to the Bishop of Durham's attack on a miraculous view of the resurrection. In order to safeguard his overall purpose of creating free rational beings God performs miracles, if at all, only very rarely. It is not necessarily unfair to perform a miracle for one person rather than another if the goal of creation is more likely to be achieved that way than by performing miracles for everyone. God works his purpose in the world not only through his spirit but through his incarnate life. This safeguards our freedom and allows God to influence us on our terms, at our level. Christ is unique: but his uniqueness exists to bring about the salvation of all people. Any miracles connected with him have to be seen in that light. It may be only a few involved in their immediate effects but their ultimate purpose is to embrace everyone.

The first point made in answer to the Bishop's views was that the question he raises is just as relevant to his own understanding of the resurrection as it is to those who believe in the empty tomb. Both views involve a miracle. Some attempt has been made to suggest why it is that God might act miraculously in Christ but not work miracles for those in Auschwitz. There yet remains the question of the type of miracle. Why should God transfigure the physical body of Jesus rather than simply assure his followers of his continuing presence? The reason is that God has a purpose not only for personal life but for matter itself. Matter itself is to be transformed. St Paul suggests as much when he writes:

> For the creation waits with eager longing for the revealing of the sons of God; for the creation was subject to futility, not of its own will but by the will of him who subjected it in hope; because the creation itself will be set free from its bondage to decay and obtain the glorious liberty of the children of God. (Romans 8, 19–21)

There is one immediate difficulty for modern people. On the tomb of the Marquess of Montrose, dated 1681, in

St Giles's Cathedral, Edinburgh, are the words:

> Scatter my ashes, strew them in the air.
> Lord, since thou knowest where all these atoms are
> I'm hopeful thou'lt recover once my dust
> And confident thou'll raise me with the just.

But we know that our physical body decomposes and becomes part of the earth. We find it difficult to conceive of the physical constituents being put together again in order that we can clamber out of our graves at doomsday. Apart from anything else the decomposed corpuscles of our bodies now form the bodies of other living things. So, when Paul draws a direct parallel between our resurrection and that of Christ, we cannot entirely follow him, if we believe his physical body was totally transformed. But the transformation of his body does have a crucial relationship to the destiny of the universe: it points to the transformation of matter itself.

As already mentioned Bishop Gore used to speak of 'the wonderful coherence of Christian Doctrine'. He was struck by the fact, as others have been, how the Christian faith hangs together; it is all of a piece; there is a delicate balance and mutual interaction between one part and another. This is certainly so in the Christian attitude to the material world. In the first chapter of the Book of Genesis after each aspect of creation God says, 'And God saw everything that he had made, and behold, it was very good'. In the course of its history the Church has rejected Gnosticism and Manichaeism, Marcionism and all forms of dualism; all views which would drive a wedge between the material and the spiritual, the body and the spirit. Christianity is a sacramental religion, using material forms to body forth and convey spiritual realities. Within this affirming context 'the resurrection of the body' has its natural place. The physical and material, the outward and social, is not to be lost but to be transformed. It is true that our physical bodies moulder in the grave. But Christ was raised from the dead, body and soul, and Christians are incorporate in Christ. We find our life in and through him, as part of his body. As *The Nature of Christian Belief* put it, talking about belief in the empty tomb: this belief affirms:

> that in the resurrection life the material order is redeemed, and the fulness of human nature is taken into God's eternal destiny for his creation.[18]

Again, it asserted:

> As regards belief that Christ's tomb was empty on the first Easter Day, we acknowledge and uphold this as expressing the faith of the Church of England, and as affirming that in the resurrection life the material order is redeemed, and the fulness of human nature, bodily, mental and spiritual, is glorified for eternity.[19]

What has been established so far is this. First, the resurrection of Christ's body, the transmutation of his flesh and blood into the very stuff of glory, is important from a theological point of view. It is of a piece with the whole Christian attitude to the material world. Secondly, in relation to the Bishop of Durham's points about miracles, the idea of a God who performs a unique miracle in Christ with a view to the salvation of human kind is worthy of our moral assent. The time has come to look a little more closely at how we assess evidence.

How we interpret the past will depend not only on what there is left of the past for us to interpret but our own presuppositions and interests. These vary from generation to generation and context to context. As the distinguished historian E.H. Carr wrote, history is a never ending process:

> it is a continuous process of interaction between the historian and his facts, an unending dialogue between present and past.[20]

Yet can one's interpretation of the past take place in total isolation from one's expectations and hopes about the future? An interpretation of the 1917 revolution in Russia for example will inevitably be shaped in part by one's views of the perfectibility of man, indeed by one's whole understanding of the nature and destiny of man. It is no doubt possible to recount the story of the 1917 revolution, to give a recital of events, without such wider considerations. But as soon as one tries to assess the significance of what happened (and this enters into the selection and weighing of the facts) ultimate questions about human life protrude themselves.

These wider considerations are certainly relevant to assessing the Christian claim about Christ's resurrection. Here past, present and future are intimately bound up. In chapter 4 of his letter to the Romans, Paul refers to the experience of Abraham. He sees a continuity between the God who 'calls into existence the things that do not exist' and who 'gives life to the dead': between Abraham, who believed that God could produce offspring even though both he and Sarah were old, and the raising of Jesus. Elsewhere he often refers in the same sentence to the God who raised Christ Jesus from the dead and who will raise us in the future. Again, he sees a continuity between the God who raised Christ Jesus in the past, who now raises us from the death of sin and who will give new life to our mortal bodies. In short, there is one God who creates the world *ex nihilo*, who raised Jesus, who raises us now out of sin into eternal life and who after our physical death will recreate us for eternity. How we assess the evidence of the empty tomb will depend, in part, on our present experience of being raised from sin and our future hopes for the future.

The meaning of an event in history depends upon the context in which it is seen. As a result history is subject to constant reinterpretation for time is bringing a continuously changing perspective. Already the Second World War looks different from how it did in 1946. In one hundred years' time it will inevitably look still more different. What looks to us like a life or death struggle against the Nazis might then appear as one phase in a several hundred years' struggle against communism. This means that the meaning of history as a whole can only be known at its end. Only when all is complete will each event be seen in its proper place and perspective. But history is still open. The future has yet to be made.

The really troubling question for the Christian believer is the existence of so much suffering in the world. Time and again this seems to contradict the possibility of a loving God. The Christian hope is, however, that in the end 'God will be all in all', that all obstacles to God's loving purpose will have been overcome. Then all who have lived will be able to bless God for their existence. But that is not yet. It has still to be achieved. Christians have much sympathy with the words of Karl Marx carved on his grave in Highgate Cemetry, 'Philosophers have only interpreted the world. The point is, however, to change it.' When all has, by the grace of God and human co-operation, been changed – then, from that perspective, it will be possible to see the meaning of human history; indeed to say that it has a meaning.

When all who have lived broken, futile, frustrated and cut-short lives through circumstances in part beyond their control, are able at the consummation to bless the Lord for their transformed existence and what led up to it, then there will be meaning to be seen and given thanks for. But that is not yet. Until then we live in active love and hope. But that hope is rooted in the resurrection of Christ from the dead and our own participation in his resurrection life.

It was suggested earlier that what needs interpreting are the strange facts of the empty tomb, the claim of some of the first followers of Jesus to have experienced his risen presence and the claim of the church in every age to know Christ through the scriptures, in the Eucharist, in suffering love and in the needs of others. How this is interpreted will depend in part on our own present experience and our hopes for the future. Past, present and future are bound up together and our attitude to the one will shape our attitude to the other. For example, it is not possible to look at the strange fact of the discovery of the empty tomb of Jesus and jump from that to the belief that God raised Jesus from the dead. That conclusion can only be made by someone who believes in God; in a God who acts in history; in a God who was active in the ministry of Jesus; in a God who is experienced, in however a fragmentary way, as a God who is raising us from sin and despair, and in a God who one day will redeem all that can be redeemed. The discovery of the empty tomb, however well attested, (as we have argued, it is) cannot be assessed in isolation. For example, someone who does not believe in God or a future life or has no experience of divine grace could hardly come to interpret it in terms of the resurrection of Jesus. But for someone who does believe in God, who has some experience of divine grace and who has hope that God will transfigure all things, it will not be impossible to believe that God raised Christ Jesus from the dead.

The whole question of interpretation is highlighted by the views of the Jewish Scholar Dr Pinchas Lapide. Dr Lapide, considering the resurrection of Jesus against the background of Jewish faith experiences, affirms it to be a fact of history:

> the resurrection belongs to the category of the truly real and effective occurrences, for without a fact of history there is no act of true faith. A fact which indeed is withheld from objective science, photography, and a conceptual proof, but not from the believing scrutiny of history which more frequently leads to deeper insights.[21]

Dr Lapide is surprised by the extreme scepticism of some Christian scholars:

> I cannot rid myself of the impression that some modern Christian theologians are ashamed of the material facticity of the resurrection. Their varying attempts at dehistoricising the Easter experience which give the lie to all four evangelists are simply not understandable to me in any other way . . . often it seems as if renowned New Testament scholars in our days want to insert a kind of ideological or dogmatic curtain between the pre-Easter and the risen Jesus in order to protect the latter against any kind of contamination by earthly three-dimensionality. However, for the first Christians who thought, believed and hoped in a Jewish manner, the immediate historicity was not only a part of that happening but the indispensible

precondition of the recognition of its significance for salvation.[22]

Dr Lapide is not a Christian. He does not believe Jesus to be the Jewish Messiah, still less the second person of the Trinity. He understands Jesus, in a very positive way, from the standpoint of a Jewish theology. He believes God raised Jesus from the dead in order to bring the knowledge of himself to the gentile world. Dr Lapide's work brings out sharply how our assumptions and presuppositions play a crucial role in our interpretation of the evidence. In his view many Christian scholars have presuppositions that are blinding them to the facticity of the resurrection. Yet he himself, quite rightly from his standpoint as a practising Jew, interprets Jesus in Jewish theistic categories; very positively, but still in such a way that Judaic rather than Christian categories are the controlling ones. This in turn raises our whole understanding of God. What kind of God do we believe in? For many Christians it is the willingness of God himself to share in the suffering of the world, by becoming incarnate as a human person, that helps to make the problem of suffering livable with. Can we continue to believe that there is a God of love behind the universe if that God does not go all the way towards us to the extent of sharing our anguish? It is answers to questions like these that will determine whether we take a Jewish or Christian interpretation of the resurrection of Jesus.

How we understand the resurrection, indeed whether or not we believe in it at all, depends very much on our notion of love; upon a kind of moral sensitivity to what is and what is not appropriate to a perfect love, whether or not such a perfect love exists. There is a kind of logic of love, the exploration of which is just as crucial to one's beliefs as is an examination of the New Testament. Dr Lapide presupposes this, even if he does not discuss its implications. For, after discussing the faith of Jesus and the cry of dereliction he writes:

> Only a Jew was able to cry like that, one who felt utterly abandoned and disappointed to death. And thus the resurrection of Jesus became for his disciples on that day of ruin a theological imperative which was demanded by their never completely forgotten confidence in God . . . Jesus *must* rise in order that the God of Israel could continue to live as their heavenly Father in their hearts; in order that their lives would not become God-less and without meaning.[23]

Lapide rejects the view that this is illusory wishful thinking. Whether illusion or reality we can certainly say that if there is a God of love, one who is truly love, the logic of love demands that the disciples of Jesus be assured of his risen presence.

To the fore, then, are presuppositions about the nature of love, about what God would be like if there was a God of love. Besides this, there are for our interpretation: first, the strange disconcerting discovery of the empty tomb. Secondly, the claim of the followers of Jesus to have encountered him after his death. Thirdly, the claim of the church in every age to know the spiritual presence of Christ through the scriptures, in the Eucharist, through suffering love and in the needy. Moreover, as was said earlier, how one interprets all this will be affected by one's hope for the future. These in turn will be affected by our present experience. For the God who raised Christ Jesus from the dead and who will raise us anew for eternity is a God who raises us now from the death of sin and despair. If we know something of the present raising, we are likely to be open to the possibility of a raising in the past and the future. If we know nothing of that present resurrection experience, we are hardly likely to be sympathetic to God's action in the past or the future. Austin Farrer makes the point, though in this case discussing belief in the incarnation:

In one sense Gospel history is just history, and its procedure is the same as any history's. It is the interpretation by sympathetic understanding of a web of interacting minds, with some of which, the evangelists, we are in immediate contact, with others, Christ and the Twelve, Caiphas and Pilate, in a contact not in the same way immediate. So far Gospel history is like any other history. It is different, because one of the minds, Christ's, is not merely a natural mind, and can only be understood, therefore, by a supernatural gift. There is therefore no neutral history of Christ common to unbelievers and believers. We either accept, or do not accept, the witness of the Holy Ghost. We understand the Christ who proclaimed himself the Son of God, because we understand, though but partly, what it is for Christ to be the Son of God, because we perceive ourselves to be, in him, partakers of divinity. The God incarnate is not to us an unintelligible enigma, because our existence in grace hangs upon the fringes of his incarnation. We know, on our knees, and in the depth of our heart, what Christ is, by knowing what he has made us: and we know what he has made us, by knowing what he is.[24]

In the same way, knowing something of the resurrection power of God in our own lives, we can look sympathetically at the possibility of that power at work on the third day, and in the future.

6

Tragedy and Triumph

It was suggested in the first chapter that to understand resurrection as a 'seeing' of the cross of Jesus in a new light, as a triumph of love, has great moral appeal. On this understanding resurrection is not an objective event that overturns the crucifixion. Everything happens within the minds of the disciples. They come to a new conviction that the faith and love by which Jesus lived are indeed worth living and dying by. The moral appeal of this way of understanding the resurrection is akin to the power that tragedy has over us. Since the first Greek tragedians in the 5th century BC men have observed and reflected upon the strange effect that watching tragedy has upon the audience. Logically a tragedy should make the audience feel sad or embittered. Yet a great tragedy often produces an exalting effect, a sense of the nobility and worthwhileness of life, despite everything. The effect that a great tragedy has upon an audience has been interpreted in many different ways. The account given by F.R. Leavis is the one followed here. He wrote:

> We have contemplated a painful action, involving death and the destruction of the good, admirable and sympathetic, and yet instead of being depressed

we enjoy a sense of enhanced vitality. I take this general account as granted – as recognised for sound as far as it goes.[25]

He then goes on to state that this experience does not, however, permit an indulgence in the dramatisation of one's nobly suffering self. It does not reveal the greatness of man. Rather:

The sense of heightened life that goes with the tragic experience is conditioned by a transcending of the ego – an escape from all attitudes of self-assertion. Actually the experience is constructive or creative, and involves a recognising positive value as in some way defined and vindicated by death. It is as if we were challenged at the profoundest level with the question, 'In what does the significance of life reside?' and found ourselves contemplating for an answer a view of life, and of the things giving it value, that makes the valued appear unquestionably more important than the valuer, so that significance lies, clearly and inescapably, in the willing adhesion of the individual self to something other than itself.[26]

Leavis then refers to another author writing about the World War I poet, Isaac Rosenberg:

The value of what was destroyed seemed to him to have been brought into sight only by the destruction, and he had to respond to both facts without allowing either to neutralise the other.[27]

From one point of view the Gospels can and must be read as tragedy. A man gives himself totally over to the Father's will by announcing the presence of his kingdom.

He persists in this vocation even though he foresees quite clearly that it will lead to his rejection and death. Moreover, he sees that it will also involve others in denial and betrayal. This man, this man almost universally acknowledged to be a good man, continues on what he believes to be God's path for him and is indeed rejected and killed. It seems to end all that he stood for, the rejection of the way of trust and love and hope – not only by men but by God, for there was no last minute rescue. The man dies having experienced a great sense of abandonment and dereliction.

The story of Jesus is a tragedy as sublime as any of the world's great dramas. A dramatist of skill could produce it for the stage in those terms. Yet the story of Jesus, even when considered simply as tragedy, brings about a sense of 'enhanced vitality'. This is because, in Leavis's words, it involves 'a recognising positive value as in some way defined and vindicated by death'. The value of what was destroyed is 'brought into sight only by the destruction'.

Seeing the story of Jesus as a tragedy comparable to the tragedies of the world's greatest dramatists brings out the moral appeal implicit in an understanding of the resurrection as a 'seeing' of the cross as the triumph of love. We are invited to imagine the first disciples, as a result of the cross, as a result of the destruction of Jesus, seeing with new clarity the faith and love by which he lived and for which he died; and coming to adhere to these values as being of supreme worth.

There is an inescapably tragic dimension to human life and the tragic reading of the Gospels is one that must never be neglected. For it affirms an essential aspect of human existence. It belongs to the dignity and nobility of human beings that they are capable of recognising and affirming value, even when those values appear to have nothing in the structure of the universe or the world of events to uphold or validate them. C.S. Lewis wrote towards the end of his life that even if he did not believe in a life after death he would still want to die on the side of Christ. So it is that many agnostics and atheists have been amongst the most moral and noble of human beings. They have affirmed value, even when they thought it had no metaphysical foundation.

The problem then is how to talk about the resurrection as an objective event in a way that does not cheapen human suffering and that recognises the moral appeal of the tragic experience. It is a problem that needs to be approached somewhat obliquely. A number of considerations are relevant.

First, the mood of the time in which we now live is such that we respond with recognition to the tragic, suffering element in human life. Many, if not most, of our best novelists, playwrights and painters depict a bleak world. The sombre picture they so often present impinges upon us as 'true' to the world in which we live. We are correspondingly unhappy about anything that smacks of a happy ending. We suspect it will be trite or contrived; that it will not ring true to the experience we know. This basic assumption and presupposition affects the way we read the Gospels. It is vividly expressed in a character in *The Good Apprentice*, a novel by Iris Murdoch. One of the characters is asked about his view of Christ. He replies:

I have to think of him in a certain way, not resurrection, as it were mistaken, disappointed – well, who knows what he thought. He has to mean pure affliction, utter loss, innocent suffering, pointless suffering, the deep and awful and irre-deemable things that happen to people.[28]

It is important to note that this attitude that is so much part of the prevailing mood of our time is a presupposition, is an assumption. As such it is neither true nor false. This presupposition may help to reveal aspects of the truth, indeed it does: but it is not the only perspective on existence or the only one which discloses aspects of reality. This can be brought out by contrasting the assumptions of our own age with those of another. In 1681 Nahum Tate rewrote Shakespeare's *King Lear* in order to give it a happy ending. Lear and Cordelia live happily ever after. Cordelia marries Edgar and the fool was omitted. In our time we could just about imagine someone rewriting Lear as a joke. What is amazing about Tate's version with its happy ending is that this was the version that held the stage for 150 years. For 150 years this is what theatre goers wanted to see. This desperate desire to have a happy ending to one of Shakespeare's tragedies seems to us an absurd and gross distortion. But it may be that our own reluctance to recognise anything other than what is bleak, sombre and tragic may, at some future time, be no less regarded as distorted; part of a mood of our time, and for that reason as partial for pessimism as the 18th century was for optimism.

The reasons for our predeliction for the bleak, the sombre, the pessimistic are various. But for one important element we can again look to Iris Murdoch. In her philosophical essay *The Sovereignty of Good* she makes a passionate case for adherence to the good for its own sake. At one point she writes 'all that consoles is fake'. This lapidary statement expresses well the deep suspicion of the hopeful by our generation, derived in part from

Freud's exploration of the power of wishful thinking in human life. But it is simply not true that 'all that consoles is fake.' In bereavement, when friends and family offer support this love and friendship can be enormously consoling. It is not necessary to think that the love offered or the consolation that is derived from it is false. That love is as real as anything else in life, as is the comfort in brings. Or again, if a person goes into hospital and after exhaustive tests they are told 'I'm glad to say you have not got cancer', this is greatly relieving to the hearer. But it is not fake. Indeed anyone who goes into hospital with the unshakable conviction that any good news they might hear about their condition would be false is in a bad way; certainly incapable of grasping reality. The Christian faith certainly offers consolation (though that has come to be a somewhat weak and inadequate word). It offers eternal life. The Beatitudes offer a startling series of promises. The pure shall see God, the meek shall inherit the earth, the mourners shall be comforted, the poor will own the Kingdom of Heaven and so on. Even allowing for the metaphorical and poetic language, the thrust is unmistakable. Promises are being made. These promises may be true or false, but they cannot be written off as false simply because they offer consolation. The assertion that 'all that consoles is false' is simply an assumption: one that is quite unwarranted and which if rigidly adhered to would have the effect of closing the mind to important aspects of reality. Indeed it has affinities with the delusions of the paranoid that everyone is against them.

In order to grasp the Christian faith therefore we need to be aware of and critical of the unwarranted assumptions of the age in which we live. For these assumptions have a built-in bias in favour of pessimism, defeatism and the bleak. It is perhaps necessary to go even further and raise the question whether there is not something sick, something morbid, something spiritually blighted, about this extreme reluctance to accept anything other than an extreme pessimism about human life. This is in no way to underestimate the terrible affliction inherent in human existence or the particularly tragic nature of the century in which we live. The anguish of the world continually calls into question the possibility of a God of love. The threat posed by the presence of so much suffering to the possibility of a loving God cannot be stated too strongly. Nevertheless, it is an elementary point of human psychology that some people do hug misery to themselves. They seem to feel more satisfied bathed in a cocoon of melancholy. There is a kind of spiritual reluctance in some people to grasp that all might indeed be well.

With this critical awareness about the assumptions of the age in which we live we can read the Bible and Christian tradition in a new light. First, in the Old Testament, God's blessings were understood in very tangible ways. Corn and wine and oil increasing were seen as a sign of God's favour. There was no false spiritualising. The wrong did not lie in material goods themselves but in the fact that the poor were deprived of their fair share of them. The hope was that in the Kingdom, in the reign of justice inaugurated by God himself, there would be universally shared flourishing. Secondly, in the New Testament, the breaking in of this reign is again seen in tangible ways directly related to human well being. Most obviously the Gospels are full of people being cured of sickness. Both mental and physical illness is being healed. The Gospel comes as good news: not simply a new mental attitude but a transformation of life in its entirety. What is wrong is put right; the diseased are made whole and the poor given their due. This emphasis is continued in early Christian art. Western Christians are used to endless pictures of the crucifixion of Christ. But in, for example, the early art of Christians in Egypt the cross never appears. Instead there are pictures of Christ the healer, Christ the Good Shepherd and so on. In other words the stress is on all that is life-affirming. Thirdly, in the Eastern part of the Church the emphasis has been much more on the resurrection than on the cross alone, as has been the tendency in the West. This is in no way to deny the importance of the cross or the unique consolation that God's entry into human sin and suffering can bring us. But in the West there has been a preoccupation with the cross and the atonement, to the great neglect of the Resurrection and the Holy Spirit, which are much more to the fore in the Orthodox churches of the East.

When Jesus read in the synagogue in Nazareth he chose this passage:

> The Spirit of the Lord is upon me,
> because he has anointed me to preach good news to
>   the poor.
> He has sent me to proclaim release to the captives
> and recovery of sight to the blind,
> to set at liberty those who are oppressed,
> to proclaim the acceptable year of the Lord.
>
> (Luke 4, 18–19)

When he had finished reading and all eyes were upon him he said, 'Today this scripture has been fulfilled in your hearing'. Later, when some disciples of John the Baptist came to Jesus to enquire on behalf of their master, who was in prison, whether he was the expected Messiah, Jesus told them to go back and say:

Go and tell John what you hear and see: the blind receive their sight and the lame walk, lepers are cleansed and the deaf hear, and the dead are raised up, and the poor have good news preached to them. (Matthew 11, 4–5)

It is against the background of this that the resurrection of Christ has to be seen. Jesus brought people into the Kingdom of God in which was offered them all that they could want; the ordinary, basic, so much to be desired and so often denied human blessings like food and health. Not these alone, but these indeed. Christ offered real, tangible hope.

It has been fashionable in recent years, even amongst those who stress the objective nature of the resurrection, to say that the resurrection is not a reversal of the cross; it is, rather, a revealing of its essential nature and meaning. In pictorial terms this is signified by Christ in majesty ruling from the cross: not just a bare cross signifying Christ risen, or a crucifix signifying Christ suffering, but Christ crowned and robed, reigning from the tree, signifying the triumph of suffering love as revealed by the resurrection. This is an essential aspect of the truth. The faith and hope and love which Christ incarnated and which were revealed in all their sharpness of outline by his faithfulness to death, are indeed the values which are triumphant. Nevertheless, there is an important sense in which the resurrection does reverse the judgement of the cross. For, from a worldly point of view, Christ died defeated, a failure. He was condemned to a criminal's death, a death that in the eyes of the Jews made him an enemy of God. The forces of darkness appeared to have won. Although we can and do say such things as 'the human spirit still shone in him' or 'his love was undimmed', in the brutal world, in the world of events, the person who lived in this way was condemned and killed. For all our proper admiration for those who die for what they believe, we still want to know whether the universe itself is, in the end, on the side of, or hostile to, the values we most cherish. A distinguished cabinet minister was brought up in a devout home. When he was a teenager his sister died and he lost his faith. As he put it, 'All the forces of love and prayer went down before a germ'. Those forces of love and prayer would shine out even if the world was created by some diabolical agency. But 'they went down before a germ'. And, time and again, love and prayer do go down before sickness or wickedness. But is such sickness or wickedness to have the last word? The resurrection of Christ is a triumphant affirmation that the last word belongs to God. It sometimes seems that the world is in the grip of forces hostile to human beings, as the novels of Hardy (so popular today) suggest; or if not hostile, at least the universe is totally indifferent to human suffering, as the world of Samuel Beckett seems to indicate. But the resurrection gives a totally different perspective. It reverses the apparent victories of sin and suffering. Indeed Christ himself indicated as much when he said on a number of occasions that in the coming rule of God the first would be last and the last would be first. He is the poor man, the one who brings to a head the strand of outraged innocence that runs through the Old Testament. He is the last whom God makes first. In the resurrection this last is made first on behalf of and as a sign of the making first of all other lasts.

Human values can be recognised and lived out by believer and atheist alike. Sometimes the atheist or agnostic is more dedicated to those values than the believer. But are those values simply chosen by human beings and affirmed with courage against a hostile or indifferent universe? Or are those values recognised as being inherent in a universe which one day will reveal their triumph? The resurrection affirms, despite all appearance to the contrary, that the universe is on the side of value; not just in the human spirit but in the world of events. One day health and goodness and beauty and love and life will suffuse and shape all things.

Suffering is contrary to the direct will of God. God did not will Christ to die a painful death as a young man any more than he wills the deaths of other young people. Such outrages are plainly contrary to his will.[29] The resurrection of Christ comes as a revelation of his will, as a promise of life and health and love in opposition to all that seems to destroy those values. Nevertheless, in Christian perspective, there is a mystery about suffering. For suffering can sometimes be made to contribute to the flowering of the values which the resurrection reveals as triumphant. As Edwin Muir put it so memorably, in his poem contrasting the darkened world in which we now live with the paradise of Eden:

> But famished field and blackened tree
> bear flowers in Eden never known.
> Blossoms of grief and charity bloom in these
> darkened fields alone.
>
> . . . . .
>
> Strange blessings never in paradise
> fall from these beclouded skies.[30]

The suffering of the world has produced a charity which was not known in the perfection of Eden. Strange blessings have come from the anguish of life. So it is that the resurrection can never be seen simply as a reversal of the crucifixion, however much, as we have stressed, it must also be seen in that way. It is also a revelation of the love that can come out of the experience of suffering. We cannot pretend that the suffering has never been. The resurrection cannot be such a reversal that it blots out totally all that has gone before. That would make the human story of no point. Rather, the suffering and what it has brought forth, are taken up and transfigured. So it is that the Risen Christ who appeared to Thomas had wounds that could still be seen and touched. The resplendent resurrection body of Christ was the body of his physical prime and the body of his dereliction; both were taken up, transfigured and glorified. Aquinas, in discussing the wounds in Christ's risen body, quotes Augustine: 'From these wounds . . . will shine forth a beauty which is not from the body but is the result of virtue', and himself comments, 'There even appeared in the places where the wounds were a special type of beauty'.[31]

This means that as what is healthy and flourishing in human life can act as a sign of that resurrection state in which all will be healthy and flourishing, so the transformation brought about by human suffering courageously borne can, likewise, act as a pointer to that state when all suffering will be transmuted into joy. A good example of this is given by Father H.A. Williams in his description of the painting of an old woman. He writes:

Resurrection can be seen in the portrait of an old woman by a contemporary painter of genius. The old woman's face is deeply lined as though it had been ploughed up again and again by agony upon agony. It is the face of somebody whom life has tortured without mercy. The furrows speak of wounds and deeper wounds, of sufferings and cares piled one on top of the other. It is the face of somebody who has found life an experience of continuous betrayal. The old woman looks as if no sorrow has passed her by, as though she could never be surprised again by any kind of degree of pain. Yet in his portrayal of this agonizingly tragic face, the artist has given an over-all impression of triumph. In its very lines and furrows the face gives off an invincible strength. The old woman possesses a wisdom and serenity which nothing can take from her. She is in possession of true and indestructible riches. She has looked on the travail of her soul and is satisfied. She is at peace – the peace which can belong only to those who are fully and deeply alive. What the artist has shown is victory over suffering by its acceptance – not the passive acceptance of hopeless resignation, but the active acceptance of one who has been willing to receive the suffering and absorb it and thus to make it contribute powerfully to what she is. The portrait shows somebody who has become fully a person by means of those very hammer-blows of experience which might have broken her up completely.[32]

Those who believe in the objectivity of the resurrection of Christ experience two main difficulties in conveying the reality of this belief. First, though real and thoroughly objective, the risen Christ was not and is not visible and tangible in the same way that sticks and stones are visible. Secondly, how can the resurrection be proclaimed in a way that does not undermine the truths inherent in the cross? The crucifixion is a focus and symbol of 'the deep and irremediable things that happen to human beings'. It expresses the tragic dimension to human existence. This keeps before us the reality of human suffering, in no way glossing over it or pretending it is other than it is. It also brings out the values which human beings are willing to affirm, even if the universe is meaningless, and something of the dignity and nobility of human beings in their willingness to recognise and live by those values. The resurrection of Christ, as an objective event, needs to be stated in a way which in no way cheapens the reality of human suffering or the truth implicit in the tragic dimension or the courage of pursuing that good for its own sake.

Despite these two major problems the resurrection of Christ has been explored and stated in at least two modern novels in such a way as to convince the reader. In Patrick White's *The Riders in the Chariot* and William Golding's *Darkness Visible* a Christ figure is raised from the dead and appears to a few people. But there is no failure of conviction between the death and the appearing. *The Riders in the Chariot* and *Darkness Visible* are strange, ambitious novels. But within the world which they depict there is no break in conviction between the visible and the invisible, the death and the rising, the tragic and the triumphant.

Yet it is perhaps above all in some pieces of music that the reality of resurrection is most successfully conveyed. For music, more than any other art form, can communicate sheer delight, can convey the sense that 'all shall be well and all manner of things shall be well'. Yet often such music is also able to incorporate, and as it were 'redeem', the dark and the tragic. For some it is above all the music of Mozart that is able to do this. Karl Barth once wrote that the music of Mozart was food and drink to him and that in his view Mozart had a place in theology, both in the doctrine of creation and in eschatology. He knew more, thought Barth, then either the early fathers of the church or the reformers, for he heard the negative only in and with the positive and never in abstraction. Similarly Ulrich Simon has said that Mozart's D minor quartet and the G minor quintet evoke in every bar the truth about God.

Again, a character in a novel by Rebecca West,[33] a talented musician, comments in a dark mood, 'What's the good of music if there's all this cancer in the world?' But someone else replies, 'What's the harm of cancer, if there's all this music in the world?' In great music cancer and all the other negatives can be taken into account but 'in and with the positive', with, a Christian might say, the resurrection. Or, we might say, music and what it is able to do is a sacrament of a deeper truth still, the resurrection and its relation to the cross. The cross is there, but only in and with the resurrection; and the music is such it is possible to say 'What's the harm of cancer?'

The Universal Hope

Myth and Fact

The hope of a significant life after death is as old as mankind; so also is the fear that death will bring only a pale version of this life or something even worse. It is instructive to look at these fears and, more particularly the hope in one of the most ancient civilisations of the world, that of Ancient Egypt. As is well known the ancient Egyptians were much concerned about what would happen after death and of this the great Pyramids are just one sign. It is untrue however to say that they were obsessed with death. Rather, they loved life and were concerned to see life after death in terms of the best that this life affords. The most important myth that developed in Ancient Egypt, one with important points of contact with the Christian story, was that of Isis and Osiris. The fullest account is given by Plutarch, the first Greek essayist, in the first century AD, but snippets of the myth, going back 2000 years before this, confirm Plutarch's version.

Osiris was ruling justly when he was killed by the malevolent Seth after a trick. Seth made a fine desk and at a banquet offered it to the person it fitted. Fellow conspirators tried the desk and found it did not fit. Osiris lay in it, was trapped, and thrown into the Nile. Osiris was recovered from the Nile by Isis but once again Seth stepped in, stole the body, chopped it up and scattered it. Isis and her sister, not to be beaten, recovered the pieces and reconstituted them by magic, Isis fluttering her wings over the body to bring Osiris to life.

The original Egyptian cult was that of the Sun God, which also offered hope of a life after death. What is interesting is that this was replaced by the Isis/Osiris myth. The reason seems to be that the latter myth, with its themes of a struggle against an evil power, and the hope of life after great suffering, including total dismemberment, met some deep-seated longing in the populace. Ra, the Sun God, offered life after death. But Isis/Osiris offered new life after terrible suffering and loss. Human life is such that it is the latter myth which met the deepest need.

The other interesting point about the Osiris story is that originally the hope of a blessed after-life may have been for the King alone. Then the hope was extended to his family and officials, who were buried in tombs round the royal burial place. Finally, the hope was extended to the population as a whole, but the resurrection of others depended in some way upon the resurrection of the king. When the dead person was buried the name Osiris was printed before their name. Resurrection was, as it were, 'in' Osiris, much as the Christian church thinks of resurrection 'in' Christ.

The hope of a significant life after death can be paralleled from almost every human culture. The Egyptian story has been selected as one striking example of the universal longing of human kind. In the 19th century it was fashionable to interpret Christian belief in the death and resurrection of Christ as just another expression of this longing, as one more example of a widely shared mythical theme. From the standpoint of Christian faith, however, it looks very different. The death and resurrection of Christ are real events that fulfil the yearnings of the myths. Christ really did die and rise again; and to this truth the myths of dying and rising gods point in their different ways.

The word myth has become so obscured by controversy it has almost lost its purpose. In the popular mind it stands for a story about the gods that has no basis in reality. In the minds of some theologians it has become a word that expresses spiritual truth but in a non-historical form. C.S. Lewis, who made a lifetime's study of the myths of the world, which he loved, and who came to believe the Christian faith as a matter of personal conviction, is perhaps as well qualified as anyone to write on the subject. He was quite clear that myth has an important role in the Christian faith, as giving a universal dimension to the particular and the historical. But he was adamant that the Christian faith did not consist of myth alone. There was a firm historical basis. Considered simply as myth, he did not find the Christian story the most appealing of those on offer. The Norse myths were what he loved. But it was the sheer facticity of the Christian faith with which he felt he had to reckon. On 19th September 1931, Lewis spent a whole night talking to his friends. Later he wrote:

What Dyson and Tolkein showed me was this: that if I met the idea of sacrifice in a Pagan story, I didn't mind it at all: again, that if I met the idea of a god sacrificing himself at himself . . . I liked it very much and was mysteriously moved by it: again, that the idea of the dying and reviving god (Balder,

Adonis, Bacchus) similarly moved me provided I met it anywhere *except* in the Gospels . . . Now the story of Christ is simply a true myth: a myth working on us in the same way as the others, but with this tremendous difference, that *it really happened*.[34]

This factual basis of Christianity was vital for Lewis and his stress on this separates him from some modern thinkers who regard myth and historical fact as mutually exclusive. But in emphasising that myth has become fact, Lewis also wanted to affirm that the mythical element or form of expression is still valuable, indeed essential.

Lewis regarded the mythical form as essential in religion because it is only myth that can give us the combined advantages of abstract and concrete thinking. When we think, we are, inevitably and properly, involved in abstractions. But when we are moved, it is by particular people or situations. How can we think and feel at the same time? How can the universal and particular be combined? Through myth, said Lewis. For myth allows us to feel and be moved. Yet at the same time it seeks to convey a truth that is universal not particular.

Lewis was willing to draw a conclusion from this line of reasoning which did not please everyone. Whilst there is a special illumination in Christianity, there is also a light that lightens every man that comes into the world.

Those who do not know that this great myth became fact when the Virgin conceived are, indeed, to be pitied. But Christians also need to be reminded that what became fact was a myth, that it carries with it into the world of fact all the properties of a myth. God is more than a god, not less: Christ is more than Balder, not less. We must not be ashamed of the mythical radiance resting on our theology. We must not be nervous about 'parallels' and 'Pagan Christs': they ought to be there – it would be a stumbling block if they weren't. We must not, in false spirituality, withhold our imaginative welcome. If God chooses to be mythopoeic – and is not the sky itself a myth? – shall we refuse to be mythopathic? For this is the marriage of heaven and earth: Perfect Myth and Perfect Fact: claiming not only our love and our obedience, but also our wonder and delight, addressed to the savage, the child and the poet in each one of us no less than to the moralist, the scholar, and the philosopher.[35]

Lewis was willing to go even further than this. Despite all his insistence on the factual basis of Christianity he thought that the myth itself (whether or not related to the fact) could nourish religious life. A man who disbelieved the Christian story as fact but continually fed on it as myth would, perhaps, be more spiritually alive than one who assented and did not think much about it.

Immortal Diamond

The resurrection of Jesus Christ offers hope for the resurrection of every person. As the Nicene Creed puts it, 'We look for the resurrection of the dead', or as the Apostles Creed states the matter, 'I believe in . . . the resurrection of the body'. According to the schema that held the field for most of Christian history, there are two states in our transition to immortality. First, when we die, our immortal souls slough off our outworn bodies.

Secondly, at Christ's coming again in glory, the dead will be raised and their souls will be joined with glorified bodies. This traditional schema has come under various forms of attack.

First, the whole concept of soul has been denied both philosophically and theologically. But from a philosophical point of view there has in recent years been more of a comeback for 'soul talk'; not to describe a box inside a box inside a box but to indicate the unique, irreducible significance of the human person. Talk about soul is part of a holistic way of looking at human persons. It denies that soul is identical with brain and that persons are identical with chemical processes. Human persons are capable of thought and love, choice and prayer and talk of soul brings out the significance of such aspects, aspects which cannot be explained in purely biochemical, neurological or psychological language. From the theological point of view the notion of soul has been attacked as a Greek import into Christianity. The Hebrews thought of human beings in psychosomatic terms, as a unity of body, mind and spirit. So, it is suggested, do we; and on this view any talk of soul is harmful for it encourages a dualism of soul and body. Now, it is undoubtedly true that the Hebrew feel for the psychosomatic unity of man fits helpfully with the predominant 20th century view. But the divine revelation is not limited to Hebrew or 20th century forms of thought. The concept of the soul certainly appears in the Bible, especially in the Apocrypha. Jesus made popular views of the soul his own, as when he said to the penitent thief, 'Today thou shalt be with me in paradise', and a concept which the Church made its own and taught for 1500 years is not lightly to be dismissed. It seems worth retaining soul language therefore to point up a holistic view of the person and to underline the irreducible nature of personhood. So, if that is the function of soul language, what is the function of talk about resurrection of the body?

The phrase 'resurrection of the body' expresses the faith and hope that after death we will be more fully and richly ourselves than we are now. So many pictures of the after-life have suggested that it is a place to be avoided at all costs; a place where the life we live is literally only a shadow of the life we live now; a wispy half-life. Hope in the resurrection of the body is hope that our experience as a physical being was not just a temporary phase to be enjoyed or endured to death but part of our essential being. Our physical experiences will be taken up and transformed and our capacity for sensual enjoyment will be enlarged, albeit in a way which could also be called spiritual. Most human beings have a sense of envy when they see birds wheeling and gliding in the air. We are so bound by our bodies but birds seem so much more able to make the environment yield to them. Perhaps this nostalgia for flying is a haunting echo of some final state when our spiritual body experiences total freedom. It is something of this that Thomas à Kempis pointed to in his hymn:

O how glorious and resplendent,
Fragile body, shalt thou be,
When endued with so much beauty,
Full of health, and strong, and free,
Full of vigour, full of pleasure
That shall last eternally.[36]

The traditional scheme presented us with two stages; first death, which freed the soul from its mortal body, and secondly, the resurrection of the dead in which the soul was united with a glorified body. There are two main difficulties about this picture. First, we find it difficult to imagine a naked soul without any means of expressing itself. Secondly, we know that our bodies become part of the earth and are continuously recycled as part of the process of nature. If our physical corpuscles were resurrected at the end of time, of whose body would they form a part? For this reason, as was suggested in an earlier chapter, there is one important difference between Christ's resurrection and ours and therefore one point in which we must differ from Paul's view of the matter. For in 1 Corinthians 15 Paul draws a straightforward parallel between Christ's resurrection and ours. But this cannot be so. Instead Christ's resurrection is a sign of the resurrection of the whole material order at the end of time. This said, and any view of the resurrection of physical corpuscles thus rejected, there is something in the traditional schema that needs to be safeguarded, which is this. The Christian hope is not simply about the future of particular individuals but about the future of the whole universe and the future of particular individuals is intimately bound up with the future of the whole creative process. St Paul sensed this and expressed it in his famous words, already quoted earlier:

For the creation waits with eager longing for the revealing of the sons of God; for the creation was subject to futility, not of its own will but by the will of him who subjected it in hope; because the creation itself will be set free from its bondage to decay and obtain the glorious liberty of the children of God. We know that the whole creation has been groaning in travail together until now; and not only the creation, but we ourselves, who have the first

114

fruits of the spirit, groan inwardly as we wait for
adoption as sons, the redemption of our bodies.
(Romans 8, 19–22)

Teilhard de Chardin expressed the same sense of the
eager longing of all creation in his visionary writings on
the evolutionary process.

Hope for the resurrection of the body, as far as the
individual is concerned, is hope that our real self, the self
known only to God, will be recreated in a form and
manner appropriate to an eternal mode of existence; in
that existence we will be more, not less, fully ourselves.
The question 'Who am I?' admits of no easy answer. Am
I the self I was at 8 or 38 or 88? Am I the self I was in my
prime or the self when I have gone senile? The Christian
answer is that the person we are is known fully only to
God. Moreover, although at death we may go out into the
dark and know nothing, God continues to know us. Our
knowledge may cease but God does not forget us; and
this essential self he clothes with a means of expression
appropriate to eternity, as once he clothed us with a
means of expression, flesh and blood, appropriate to a
mortal existence.

To think of two stages, at death and at the end of the
universe, is to think in terms of time. But both stages are
enclosed within the eternity of God. This reminds us that
we are not so much dealing with a temporal sequence, as
using language metaphorically to indicate truths that no
single metaphor can safeguard. Soul talk alerts us to the
unique self which is each one of us, not reducible to its
constituent parts, and known fully to God alone.
Resurrection of the body talk expresses the hope that this
self, known to God, will be recreated by him in a form
appropriate to an eternal mode of existence, an existence

in which we will flourish as never before. Talk of all this happening when Christ returns in glory to raise the living and the dead at the end of time expresses the conviction that it is not solitary individuals whom God wishes to redeem: he has a purpose for the whole and our future and the future of the whole are intimately bound up. Gerard Manley Hopkins puts it in these words:

> Enough! The Resurrection,
> A heart's-clarion! Away grief's gasping, joyless days, dejection,
>   Across my foundering deck shone
> A beacon, an eternal beam. Flesh fade, and mortal trash
> Fall to the residuary worm; world's wildfire, leave but ash:
>   In a flash, at a trumpet crash,
> I am all at once what Christ is, since he was what I am, and
> This Jack, joke, poor potsherd, patch, matchwood, immortal diamond,
>   Is immortal diamond.[37]

The world in which we live seems so solid and such speculations seem so fantastical. But is the world so solid? Scientists tell us that what we call matter is mostly nothing, just empty space. When they penetrate that space they find patterns of energy that are only mathematically describable, quarks, gluons and other strange sounding entities. The Quantum world which modern science and maths has opened up to us is a very strange world indeed. Who knows whether there may not be other worlds, invisible to us, but no less real, intersecting with ours? Other patterns of energy but not describable even in mathematical terms? Such, certainly, is the Christian faith. Austin Farrer has written:

Heaven, then, is a created sphere where God bestows his presence by his action, especially his action through heart and mind. And where is heaven? When I was a lad it was still supposed to be an insoluble problem. If heaven is completely non-spatial, then (we used to say) the heavenly life must be a featureless sea of feeling, a shapeless ecstasy; or anyhow, nothing you could fairly call the resurrection-state of man. Whereas if heaven has any form of spatial dimension, then it falls somewhere in the field of space; a telescope might record it, an astronaut might reach it. And so heaven is pulled back into the perishable universe.

A pretty puzzle, and I was amazed to hear it solemnly restated the other day by a professor of philosophy; for I had supposed that Einstein had shown it up once for all as a piece of nonsense. According to his unanswerable reasoning, space is not an infinite pre-existent field or area in which bits of matter float about. Space is a web of interactions between material energies which form a system by thus interacting. Unless the beings or energies of which heaven is composed are of a sort to interact physically with the energies in our physical world heaven can be as dimensional as it likes, without ever getting pulled into our spatial field, or having any possible contact with us of any physical kind. There may well be contacts which are not physical at all between earthly minds and heavenly minds, but that's another story. How I wish we could explain the Einsteinian theory to St Augustine! Obviously his heaven is dimensional; but the stuff of glory which composes its constituents is surely not apt to interact with sticks and stones, with flesh and blood.[38]

C.S. Lewis approached the question another way. He argued, it is not matter as such that really concerns us but our sensations. What the soul cries out for is the resurrection of the senses. Matter only counts for us because it is the source of our sensations. And we already have some feeble and intermittent power of raising dead sensations from the grave through memory. Memory brings the past into the present. By that Lewis did not mean that the dead will simply have the power of remembering earthly sensations, rather the other way round. Our memory now is but a foretaste, a mirage even, of a power which the soul will exercise hereafter. There will, however, be two differences. Our power to recall the past will not come and go but will be permanent. Secondly memory will not be private. I can now tell you about the vanished fields of my childhood only imperfectly and in words. Then I will be able to take you for a walk through them. It's a mistake, thought Lewis, to dismiss memories as being inferior to the original experience. If we went back to the wheatfield we might see stalks of grain bearing grass. It is the transfiguring power of memory that remembers our visits as 'orient and immortal wheat', to use Traherne's words. This power of memory to glorify the past is the beginning of resurrection. This resurrection state may not happen all at once. We may first have to go to Lenten lands to be made ready but one day we will recover, in transfigured, glorified form, what time has borne away.

Then the new earth and sky, the same and yet not the same as these, will rise in us as we have risen in Christ. And once again, after who knows what aeons of the silence and the dark, the birds will sing out and the waters flow, and lights and shadows move across the hills and the faces of our friends laugh upon us with amazed recognition.

Guesses, of course, only guesses. If they are not true, something better will be. For we know that we shall be made like Him, for we shall see Him as He is.[39]

Seeking us in hell

The resurrection of Christ is not just for a few selected individuals. It is a fact in which the whole universe is grounded and by which all human beings are upheld. In Western art pictures of the resurrection are somewhat disappointing. They usually depict a solitary Christ standing on a flat grave, clad in a white robe and holding a banner. In Eastern art, however, the scene is much more dramatic and also more theologically profound. For Christ is shown raising humanity with him. The picture on the cover of this book, a reproduction of a fresco from the church of the Chora (Kariye in Turkish) in Istanbul shows Christ being raised with Adam in his right hand and Eve in his left hand. Adam and Eve are not, of course, ordinary figures. They are the parents of the whole human race and like the whole human race both made in the image of God and fallen from grace. In raising Adam and Eve Christ raises humanity. In the picture the other figures behind Eve are St Stephen and the Apostles. Behind Adam are the prophets and Kings of the Old Testament. But it is the raising of Adam and Eve that is of greatest significance because from them spring forth not just those of the old and new covenant but all people.

This theme needs to be taken with another that is no less strong in Eastern Theology, the descent of Christ to the abode of the departed or, as we say, his descent into hell. It is a theme that is to the fore on Holy Saturday in the Byzantine rite. Here for example, are three verses from the Mattins of that day:

> To earth hast thou come down, O Master, to save Adam, and not finding
> him on earth, thou hast descended into hell, seeking him there.
> Uplifted on the Cross, thou has uplifted with thyself all living men;
> and then descending beneath the earth thou raisest up all that lie buried there.
> The whole creation was altered by thy Passion; for all things suffered
> with thee, knowing, O Lord, that thou holdest all in unity.

This theme is not entirely absent in Western Theology: it is for example present in William Langland's *Piers Plowman* where Christ descends to hell and his secret words are heard, 'My righteousness and my justice shall rule over hell . . . I should be an inhuman king if I refused to help my own brethren'. Also in Julian of Norwich who talks of Christ going into hell where 'he raised up the great root out of the deep darkness, which rightfully was knit to him in high heaven'.[40]

The eternal Son of God has become the brother of every human being, even those in the hell of self-absorption, despair or sin, whether that hell is now or hereafter. He is the brother of all those in hell, and though himself without sin, has entered that hell on their behalf. A number of writers at the Reformation thought of Christ entering hell during the period of dereliction, when on the cross he cried out, 'My God, My God, why hast thou forsaken me?' Christ has entered hell and in being raised from the dead he raises from hell all his brethren who are willing to allow themselves to be pulled up by his strong outstretched arms. He is raised from the dead and hell is raised with him. 'The whole creation was altered by thy passion' goes the Mattins verse. And not least, our whole perspective is altered. For whatever appearances to the contrary, there is a pillar of hope at the heart of the universe.

When we look at the world about us and follow its sad and tragic stories in the media we are often appalled and numbed at what is happening. Faith is tested to the limit. But there is a mystic fact which alters everything, the death and resurrection of Christ. The universe is literally founded upon and grounded in his passion and rising again. He has entered hell and rejoined those in hell to the creative source of their existence and nothing can finally defeat that love or break that union. Heaven and earth are joined never to be unjoined. God and man are bound never to be unbound. For Christ is one with his brethren even when they are in hell, and entering hell he has raised humanity to heaven.

Many in the modern world are rightly concerned about facts. It is facts which distinguish truth from falsehood, reality from illusion. But for a Christian the whole concept of a fact takes on a new dimension. The death and resurrection of Christ is the fact of facts; the fact in which all other facts are rooted.

The Last shall be First

The whole universe in some sense depends upon the passion and rising again of Christ. But this does not mean that there is some automatic entry into the life to come for everyone. On the contrary, nothing is more clear and stark from the Bible, that there is a division. In short the eternal kingdom of glory belongs to the poor.

When we look at the world so much in it seems to deny the existence of God. The people of the Old Testament had this sense, strongly, but instead of resigning themselves to an agnosticism they looked forward to the day when God would act to put right all that is wrong, thereby revealing that he is indeed real and in charge of events. In particular the Old Testament focuses on the way the poor are exploited and oppressed. The word poor is a complex word. It includes physical poverty but goes beyond it to indicate a spiritual attitude; the attitude which pins its hopes on nothing in this world but entirely on God; an attitude of total trust in God. So when people in the Old Testament looked forward to the time when God would decisively act and intervene in the affairs of the world to put right what is wrong and establish his just rule, they thought in particular of God acting on behalf of the poor person who, oppressed by the world, puts his total trust in God. This theme is particularly poignant in the Psalms where the poor person, the violated innocent one, cried out to God for vindication. One of the most important aspects of the New Testament is that Christ makes this theme his own. He is God's poor person; the violated innocent one. He puts his total trust in his Father and is brutally rejected and crucified by the world.

122

This reality is incarnate in his person and present in his teaching. For at the heart of the teaching is his announcement that the long expected rule of God in human affairs, the Kingdom of God, is present; that God is acting so that the first will be last and the last will be first. The Kingdom of God, said Jesus, belongs to the poor, the meek, those who mourn, those who suffer. These last will be first in the great reversal of the world's scale of values brought about by the Kingdom.

In the resurrection God vindicated the poor person, the violated innocent one. He made the last first and brought in his kingdom. The Kingdom belongs to Christ, the poor person, and all those poor with whom he has united himself. At the end of the Roman Catholic Wedding Mass the new couple are blessed in the following words:

> May you always bear witness to the love of God in
> this world
> so that the afflicted and the needy
> will find in you generous friends
> and welcome you into the joys of heaven.

The Kingdom of God belongs to the poor – and their friends. The poor welcome their friends into the joys of heaven.

Hope for this World and the next

The Christian hope of a resurrected order, which was once so central to its proclamation has experienced devastating criticism during the last 150 years. Both Marx and Freud, to mention just two, subjected it to important moral criticism. In short they said that the Christian hope of a heavenly world encouraged resignation in the poor, who ought to be up and struggling for their just rights on this earth, and complacency in the rich. During the last three decades there have been a number of theologies which sought to do justice both to the struggle for better conditions on earth and the basic Christian truths. Moltmann's *Theology of Hope*, Teilhard de Chardin's *The Phenomenon of Man* and various liberation theologies from South America have tried to combine hope for real progress in social conditions on this earth with hope in a reality beyond this world; and they have tried to affirm the latter only in such a way as the struggle for justice on this earth was affirmed not undermined.

On the surface there seems a total incompatibility between hope for progress on this earth (whether in its Marxist or any other form) and the New Testament hope of 'a new heaven and a new earth'. One stresses the human effort and struggle that will bring about the kingdom of justice on earth, the other stresses God's action in bringing about that which is totally new. The one is about improvement in earthly conditions, the other about a reality that transcends space and time. Yet the incompatibility is more apparent than real. First, the Christian would want to stress that all lasting good is the work of God in and through us and that it is only by opening ourselves to the grace of God that lasting good will come about. The Kingdom of God at the end of time is indeed brought about by the action of God. But, for a Christian, it is the action of that same God to whom he seeks to open himself here and now, and who alone is the source of any lasting good. Secondly, although all that we work for here on earth seems to perish it is the very essence of belief in the resurrection, that it does not. Rather, what is good is treasured, raised up and transformed by God in the resurrecton. Furthermore, resurrection implies that there is something to be raised.

If there is no achievement on earth, then there is nothing to be resurrected. Resurrection is a transformation of what is there; so there must be something worthwhile there to be raised. The Vatican's document *Libertatis Conscientia* writing about the resurrection says:

This hope does not weaken commitment to the progress of the earthly city, but rather gives it meaning and strength. It is of course important to make a careful distinction between earthly progress and the growth of the Kingdom, which do not belong to the same order. Nonetheless, this distinction is not a separation; for man's vocation to eternal life does not suppress but confirms his task of using the energies and means which he has received from the Creator for developing his temporal life.

Enlightened by the Lord's Spirit, Christ's Church can discern in the signs of the times the ones which advance liberation and those that are deceptive and illusory. She calls man and societies to overcome situations of sin and injustice and to establish the conditions for true freedom. She knows that we shall rediscover all these good things – human dignity, fraternal union and freedom – which are the result of efforts in harmony with God's will, 'washed clean of all stain, illumined and transfigured when Christ will hand over to the Father the eternal and universal kingdom', which is a Kingdom of freedom.

The vigilant and active expectation of the coming of the Kingdom is also the expectation of a finally perfect justice for the living and the dead, for people of all times and places, a justice which Jesus Christ, installed as supreme judge, will establish. This promise, which surpasses all human possibilities, directly concerns our life in this world. For true justice must include everyone; it must bring the answer to the immense load of suffering borne by all the generations. In fact, without the resurrection of the dead and the Lord's judgement, there is no justice in the full sense of the term. The promise of the resurrection is freely made to meet the desire for true justice dwelling in the human heart.

This is a balanced statement, which is dependent on no particular theology of hope or liberation (though quite compatible with either) and of particular importance are the words:

She knows that we shall rediscover all these good things – human dignity, fraternal union and freedom – which are the result of efforts in harmony with God's will, 'washed clean of all stain, illumined and transfigured when Christ will hand over to the Father the eternal and universal kingdom'.

St Paul wrote to the Christians at Corinth, 'Your labour in the Lord is not in vain'. It is not in vain because it is known and treasured by God and will be raised and transformed to make the bricks of the eternal kingdom. The Kingdom of God soars beyond space and time into the heaven of heavens, but the bricks of that kingdom have to be made and laid on earth. When they are so laid, they require the resurrection in order to meet the demand for true justice. As *Libertatis Conscientia* put it:

Homer, Richard - "Christ Rex". 1937. Cassorp.

at fcc 83.

p.37 Discourse of ignorance & p.82 — truth not apprecianza
& Cohe of Galilee? (reference to him having "already
appeal & left" could be a misreading of Nazara text

p.79 f. Discussion of why miracles could be selective
p.83 meaning of history only known at the end
p.97 Analysis of our ancient age of dispair

p. with Rev. (common.
here we are raising "darkness visible".

p.112 the concept of the soul

n 6. p 114 from a the recognition of the universe - not just individual ic. The place of the material.

For true justice must include everyone; it must bring the answer to the immense load of suffering borne by all the generations. In fact, without the resurrection of the dead and the Lord's judgement, there is no justice in the full sense of the term. The promise of the resurrection is freely made to meet the desire for true justice dwelling in the human heart.

The pledge of that promise is the resurrection of Jesus Christ from the dead, the first fruits of the resurrection of all the dead.

Notes

1. Stevie Smith, 'An Agnostic', *Collected Poems*, Allen Lane, 1978, p.347
2. Geza Vermes, *Jesus the Jew*, SCM, 1973, p.41
3. For different accounts of what happened see Acts 22, 4–16 and Acts 26, 9–18
4. Cuthbert Bardsley & William Purcell, *Him we declare*, Mowbrays, 1976, p.74
5. Leslie Hunter, *John Hunter, D.D.: A Life*, Hodder & Stoughton, 1921, p.104
6. Dietrich Bonhoeffer, *Life Together*, SCM, 1976, p.62
7. James Barr, 'Fundamentalism & Biblical Authority' in *Heaven & Earth — Essex Essays in Theology & Ethics*, Andrew Linzey & Peter Wexler, Ed., Churchman, 1986, p.29
8. ARCIC, CTS/SPCK 1982, Para 7
9. Oscar Wilde, '*De Profundis*', *Selected Essays & Poems*, Penguin, 1954, p.162
10. *Ibid.*, p.179
11. *Luther: Letters of Spiritual Counsel*, T.G. Tappert, Ed., SCM, 1955, p.240
12. Malcolm Muggeridge, *Something Beautiful for God*, Fount, 1972, p.74
13. *Ibid.*,
14. William Blake, 'A Vision of the Last Judgement', in *Complete Works*, G.L. Keynes, Ed., OUP, p.652
15. Thomas Traherene, 'Wonder', *Centuries, Poems & Thanksgivings*, H.M. Margoliouth, Ed., Vol 11, OUP, 1958, p.7
16. William Blake 'The Marriage of Heaven & Hell', *William Blake*, J. Bronowski, Ed., Penguin, 1964, p.101
17. Francis Thompson, 'The Kingdom of God', *The New Oxford Book of Christian Verse*, OUP, 1981, p.256
18. *The Nature of Christian Belief*, Para 50, Church House

Publishing, 1986

19. *Ibid.*, Para 3
20. E.H. Carr, *What is History?* Penguin, 1981, p.30
21. Pinchas Lapide, *The Resurrection of Jesus*, SPCK, 1984, p.92
22. *Ibid.*, p.130
23. *Ibid.*, pp.88/89
24. Austin Farrer, 'History & the Gospel' in *A Celebration of Faith*, Hodder & Stoughton, 1970, pp.44/45
25. F.R. Leavis, *The Common Pursuit*, Penguin, 1963, pp.127, 132
26. *Ibid.*, pp.127, 132
27. *Ibid.*,
28. Iris Murdoch, *The Good Apprentice*, Chatto & Windus, 1985, p.147
29. The contrary impression in the Gospels is created by the references direct or assumed, to passages in the Old Testament which suggest that the servant of God will suffer. The first Christians, seeing these passages and knowing that Jesus *had* suffered, believed it must all have been foreordained and willed by God.
30. Edwin Muir, 'One Foot in Eden', *Collected Poems*, Faber, 1960, p.227
31. Thomas Aquinas, *Summa Theologica*, 3a.54, 4
32. H.A. Williams, *The True Resurrection*, Mitchell Beazley, 1972, p.145
33. Rebecca West, *The Fountain Overflows*, Virago, 1984.
34. C.S. Lewis, *God in the Dock*, Fount, 1979, pp.44–45
35. *Ibid.*,
36. Translated by J.M. Neale, English Hymnal 431
37. Gerard Manley Hopkins, 'That Nature is a Heraclitean Fire and of the Comfort of the Resurrection', *The Poems of Gerard Manley Hopkins*, W.H. Gardner & N.H. MacKenzie, Ed., OUP, 1970, p.105
38. Austin Farrer, *Saving Belief*, Hodder & Stoughton, 1964, pp.144–145
39. C.S. Lewis, Prayer: *Letters to Malcolm*, Fountain, 1977, p.124
40. These references are discussed by Donald Allchin, *The Dynamic of Tradition*, DLT, 1981, Chapter 6

A Select Reading List
for more detailed Study

A.M. Ramsey, *The Resurrection of Christ*, Fontana 1961

Helpfully brings out the particular theology of the different Gospel writers.

C.F. Evans, *Resurrection and the New Testament*, SCM 1970

Comprehensive analysis of the developing traditions on the resurrection arguing that the empty tomb story is late in that development.

Willi Marxsen, *The Resurrection of Jesus of Nazareth*, SCM 1970

Considers what 'seeing' means and argues for the resurrection as 'mental conversion'.

Wolfart Pannenberg, *Jesus God and Man*, SCM 1968

Interesting argument for the view that the tomb was empty and the appearances were objective visions.

Raymond E. Brown, *The Virginal Conception and Bodily Resurrection of Jesus*, Paulist Press 1973

Raymond E. Brown, *The Gospel According to John*, Vol. 2, Geoffrey Chapman 1978

The Biblical sections in *Christ is Risen* are indebted to these two works by Raymond Brown.

Gerald O'Collins, *Jesus Risen*, Darton, Longman and Todd, 1987

A discussion of the views of some major modern theologians on this question.

Opening doors to the World of books

Book Tokens

Book Tokens can be bought and exchanged at most bookshops